Chains and Dollars: The Slave Business in Middle Tennessee, Part 1

By

CL Gammon

Deep Read Press

LAFAYETTE, TENNESSEE
deepreadpress@gmail.com

First Deep Read Press Edition.

Edited by: Kim Gammon

Cover Design by: Kim Gammon

Cover Photo by: Kim Gammon

Paperback ISBN: 978-1-954989-66-5

Published by:
DEEP READ PRESS
Lafayette, Tennessee
www.deepreadpress.com
deepreadpress@gmail.com

For my brother Jeff.

Other Local History Titles by CL Gammon

You can find all the local history titles listed below at Amazon or at the Deep Read Press website.

A Quarter Century of Macon County Crime (1960-1984)

Ballyhoo: John Butler and the Monkey Trial

Bizarre Murders in Tennessee: 13 True Stories

Blood on the Cumberland: The Battle of Hartsville

Death on the Highland: Spanish Flu in Macon County

Dixie Witches: 9 True Southern Witch Trials

Hanging the Macon County Witch

Highland Rim Warriors: Macon County Tennessee and World War II

Murder, Mayhem, and Moonshine: True Macon County Crime Stories

Revenue Raiders: Macon County's Whiskey War

Shallow Graves and Shattered Dreams: Solving the Murders of Three Macon County Men

The Fountain of Youth at Red Boiling Springs, Tennessee, Part 1

The Fountain of Youth at Red Boiling Springs, Tennessee, Part 2

The Macon County Race War

Tiger Strong! Macon County Football, 2024

Contents

Introduction

Money is at the root of all evil. Slavery is an evil. Therefore, money is at the root of slavery.

Slavery in the United States was a major business. A horrible business to be sure, but a business all the same. In order to understand the many facets of slavery, it must first be understood as a business.

The business of slavery did not begin in the United States, or even in the Western world. Since the first time that one group of humans gained the power to lord over another group, there has been slavery. Certainly, there have been nuances to how slavery has been practiced, but the goal of slavery has always been the same – profiting from the sweat of others without giving them an opportunity to have any control over their own lives.

Being free, even if impoverished, is superior to slavery. A poor person has the opportunity to improve his lot; a slave doesn't. A successful slave is one who gets enough to eat, doesn't feel the lash too often, and maybe every once in a while, gets to toil indoors away from the searing heat and bitter cold. But that isn't much to recommend slavery, is it?

This volume employs short paragraphs and articles to look at the business of slavery in Middle Tennessee between 1812 and 1825. It concentrates on the individuals that held and profited from slaves. Special emphasis is given to those that held a few slaves and their efforts to use and market them. Additionally, this book looks at the pains that slaveholders went to in their efforts to get back their stolen or runaway slaves.

The descriptions of slaves listed here come from slaveholders or law enforcement officials. Since they were given to make it easier to identify runaway slaves, they were quite accurate.

The same can be said for the many examples of slaveholders charactering slaves as being intelligent and literate. The characterizations were proof that slaveholders understood that slaves weren't really inferior to them.

Some of the more brutal aspects of the slave industry were never hidden. For instance, sometimes slaveholders listed scars from lashings, or marks made with branding irons, as identifying marks on runaway slaves. The fact that the movements of slaves were severely restricted was also clear for everyone to see.

Some of the individuals mentioned in this book became famous and some of them were wealthy and powerful. However, most slaveholders weren't too rich or too famous. In fact, there were those that took on slaves and then found that they couldn't afford them. They then had to either sell their slaves or hire them out for cash.

Plantations are often thought of as a large, sprawling areas worked by hundreds of slaves. However, most of the plantations mentioned in this volume were really just average sized farms where a few slaves worked.

The contention that the slave population was happy and content is a myth. The proof is in the fact that hundreds of slaves in Middle Tennessee and thousands throughout the Slave States that escaped each year.

Escapes were so common that some newspapers developed an image to be added to advertisements dealing with runaway slaves. The image showed a Black man carrying a stick over his shoulder with a handkerchief holding his meager belonging tied to the end of it. The same basic image was later used to indicate hobos.

Slaveholders often expressed their belief that runaway slaves had received help from white people. While this was sometimes true, more often than not, the slaveholders were just being paranoid.

Not everyone in Tennessee supported slavery, Over the period covered in this volume, the Tennessee legislature received petitions signed by hundreds of citizens and groups asking for either the emancipation of individual slaves, or requesting the legislature abolish slavery in the state altogether. Most of the petitions weren't acted upon, but a few of them were.

It should be noted that the accounts of runaway slaves, and slave sales listed here is by no means comprehensive. The author presents just the tip of the iceberg. Yet enough is presented to give the reader an understanding of the slavery business in Middle Tennessee.

It should also be noted that while this book deals mainly with Middle Tennessee, other sections of the state, and other states are mentioned as well.

Slaveholders are often portrayed as sycophants brandishing whips and beating slaves for nothing more than the perverse pleasure they gained from it. While there were cases of that happening, many slaveholders expressed compassion – after a fashion – for their slaves. Some of them tried to make sure that the slave families they sold were kept together. Others refused to sell slaves to speculators, and they would only sell them to those that promised to treat the slaves well. Of course, there was no way to ensure how slaves were treated once they were sold.

The question then becomes: If one was truly compassionate, why not simply free his slaves? The answer is complicated.

Even if one wasn't interested in profiting from slave labor, freeing slaves wasn't a simple task. Under Tennessee law, a slaveholder couldn't just set a slave free. It took an act of the legislature to make it happen. The process of emancipating an individual slave could be long, costly, and discouraging. A good many slaveholders simply weren't up to the task of going through the ordeal involved with emancipating their slaves.

Then, there was the worry that freed slaves might not be able to earn enough to feed themselves. Slaveholders often feared that if they set their slaves free, the newly liberated people would be left in worse conditions than they were when they were slaves. While nothing is actually worse than slavery, at the time, the myth was that being a slave was better than being a free Black person. Some historians continue to perpetuate that myth today.

Perhaps the greatest disincentive to freeing slaves, other than the financial ones, came from some segments within the white community. Some slaveholders didn't want any slaves set free, because they were worried that if a rash of slaveholders freed their slaves, the legislature might decide that slavery didn't benefit Tennessee. If that happened, then total abolition of slavery might be the next step. These slaveholders claimed that freeing slaves, even a few of them would cause an economic catastrophe in Tennessee. They didn't provide proof; their loud rhetoric was enough.

Those opposed to freeing any slaves also warned that it would lead to a slave uprising. Either, so they said, the newly freed slaves would organize those still in bondage, or those slaves not freed would long for liberty and rise in rebellion on their own.

A high percentage of poor whites also opposed ending slavery. One reason for this was social status. Even though they would never have enough money to purchase a slave themselves, they felt socially superior to slaves. After all, they reasoned, even if they were miserable, they enjoyed benefits, such as freedom of movement, that slaves never could.

There were also financial considerations that caused poor whites to want to keep slaves in bondage. The poor whites who were already struggling to feed themselves working as day laborers didn't want any competition from any additional free Black people.

The arguments against freeing slaves had no foundation in fact, but they were still powerful enough to discourage many slaveholders from liberating those they had in bondage.

1812

August 22, 1812. Slaves were such a commodity that they were often used in lieu of cash, especially during those times when legal tender was hard to come by. Below is an example.

Samuel Jackson was selling a large estate in two tracts on the north side of the Cumberland River less than seven miles from Nashville. The land adjoined the town of Haysboro.

The first tract consisted of more than 900 acres with about 200 acres cleared and the rest wooded. The property included a two-story brick house that was 50 feet across the front, a wood framed kitchen of 20 feet by 18 feet, a cedar-log barn 60 feet by 20 feet, a smokehouse, and a stone spring house. It also boasted an apple orchard, and a peach orchard.

The second tract was 400 acres of which 110 were cleared. A log cabin, a kitchen, and a smokehouse sat on it.

The land was highly prized and valuable. Jackson required payment in cash, or slaves, or both.

Sources: *The Nashville Whig*, September 2, 1812; *The Nashville, Banner*, February 10, 1912.

Note: Haysboro (also spelled Haysborough) was a town in Davidson County. It ceased to exist sometime after 1839.

September 9, 1812. Slaveholders who needed cash would sometimes sell their slaves, and at other times they would hire them out to those who needed them for a season, or a year.

A slaveholder in Nashville let it be known that he had a slave that was a good carpenter. The slaveholder was willing to sell the slave or rent him out by the month.

Source: *The Nashville Whig*, September 9, 1812.

September 15, 1812. Richard Orton was selling his property in Franklin, Tennessee. The property included two lots, a two-story house of 60 feet by 30 feet, a two-story brick kitchen, a brick smokehouse, and a dairy, a stable with 28 stalls and that was 60 feet by 30 feet, and a well with a new pump. Orton was willing to accept land or slaves as partial payment.

Source: *The Nashville Whig*, September 15, 1812.

September 25, 1812. There were a surprising number of Tennesseans who wanted to emancipate all the slaves, or failing that, to limit the slave trade within the state.

State Senator Robert C. Foster was a member of the Whig Party from Nashville. He introduced a bill to prohibit the importation of slaves into Tennessee from other states "as an article of merchandize, or for safe-keeping." The law would not apply to those who introduced slaves into the state to work on their plantations or in businesses.

On October 28, a bill passed prohibiting the importation of slaves from other states, but for only a period of five years.

Sources: *The Nashville Whig*, September 9, 1812; Black, Diane (complier). "Tennessee Senators Alphabetical Listing Individual Names." Nashville: Tennessee Library and Archives, 2010.

Note: As early as 1809, the Society of Friends (Quakers) of Jefferson County, Tennessee had petitioned the state legislature asking it to abolish slavery. Or if it wouldn't abolish slavery, at least to pass a law mandating that slave families be kept together.

Source: Office of Tennessee Secretary of State, *Tennessee Legislative Petitions*.

October 22, 1812. Someone stole a slave named Jim from Congressman Felix Grundy's plantation. Jim was 19 or 20 years of age, he stood about 5'6", and he was stoutly built.

When he left, Jim was wearing "a coarse linen shirt and pantaloons."

Grundy was certain that a convicted horse thief named James Smith had stolen Jim. Grundy further believed that Smith took Jim either into Kentucky or was hiding him in the Duck River area. Grundy offered $50 for Jim's return and another $50 for Smith's arrest and conviction. $100 was a steep price, but since Jim was worth about $400, Grundy felt he could afford it.

Source: *The Nashville Whig*, November 11, 1812.

Note: Pantaloons were close-fitting, ankle-length trousers common to that area.

Note: Felix Grundy (1877-1840) was a planter, a lawyer, and a politician. He served in the US House (1811-1814), the US Senate (1829-1838, and 1839-1840), and as the Attorney General of the United States (1838-1839).

1813

January 1, 1813. After Thomas Matherson died, his personal belongs were auctioned off at his Nashville home. Among those items sold were slaves, horses, an "elegant gig harness, iron and castings," whiskey, and two desks.

Source: *The Nashville Whig*, January 1, 1813.

January 13, 1813. John Stump, who lived on Whites Creek in Davidson County, let it be known that one of his slaves had run away. The slave, named Martin, was 20, he stood about 5'2". Martin had handsome features and was well proportioned. When spoken to, Martin tended to look down.

Stump believed that Martin would try to make his way toward the vicinity of Lexington, Kentucky. Martin grew up in Jessamine County, Kentucky about 15 miles from Lexington.

Stump didn't mention an exact figure, but he said those that captured and returned Martin, or provided information about his whereabouts, would be "well paid for their trouble."

Source: *The Nashville Whig*, January 20, 1813.

January 19, 1813. There was a slave auction at the Nashville Courthouse. After giving bonds, and the their security was approved, they had a year to pay off their purchases.

Source: *The Nashville Whig*, January 13, 1813.

February 10, 1813. Thomas W. Stocket of the Little Harpeth River area in Davidson County was in search of an experienced blacksmith. Stocket's ideal candidate would be a "sober industrious and attentive family man" who already understood the blacksmithing trade. Stocket promised to provide the blacksmith with "tools suitable for the business." Stocket also said he would provide the blacksmith with a slave to assist him. The slave had already gained eighteen months of experience helping a blacksmith.

Source: *The Nashville Whig*, January 1, 1813.

February 15, 1813. There was an auction at the Franklin City Courthouse to settle the accounts of the late L. R. Gray. Gray's estate included young slaves, horses, and an "excellent" wagon. Payment for the slaves had to be in cash. Purchasers had a year to pay off the other items.

Source: *The Nashville Whig*, January 1, 1813.

March 15, 1813. There was a major auction at Henry Jackson's plantation about a mile and a quarter north of Haysboro. Items auctioned off included cattle, horses, sheep, corn, household and kitchen furniture, and farming implements. Additionally, those slaves held by Jackson that hadn't already been sold were put on the auction block.

Source: *The Nashville Whig*, March 3, 1813.

March 26, 1813. A two-day auction on the William Ward plantation in Rutherford County began. The plantation was about two and a half miles from Abbott's Mill. Items for sale at this auction included 200 barrels of corn, 20 to 30 head of cattle, 70 to 80 hogs, sheep, and other things.

The 500-acre farm where Ward lived was also auctioned. 100 acres were cleared and a two-story 36 feet by 24 feet cedar log cabin sat on the property. The cabin had two brick chimneys and five fireplaces.

Ward also had 640 acres on Dry Fork Creek for sale. That property came with 10 slaves.

Source: *The Nashville Whig*, March 3, 1813.

April 1, 1813. A slave named Abraham, held by Captain Robert Sample of Davidson County, ran away. Abraham stood about 5'6", and he weighed between 135 and 140 pounds. He had a "very broad flat foot." He spoke rather quickly and sometimes stammered.

Word was that Abraham had used a pass written by a white man to cross the Cumberland River at Haysboro and that he still had the pass in his possession.

Captain Sample promised to "reward liberally any person" that delivered Abraham back to the plantation or jailed the slave until he could be retrieved. As of May 19, Abraham had not been returned to bondage.

Source: *The Nashville Whig*, May 12, 1813.

Note: A slave pass was a document that gave permission for a slave to travel without an escort. The penalty for a slave in possession of a forged a pass was 39 lashes.

April 14, 1813. A Nashvillian was selling two slaves. One was a man of about 40 years and the other was a little boy of about six years or so.

Source: *The Nashville Whig*, January 1, 1813.

April 27, 1813. A slave named Sam ran away from the Davidson County plantation owned by Michael Campbell. Sam was about 25, and he stood about six feet tall. He was strong and well proportioned. When describing Sam, Campbell said the runaway had a light complexion, and that he walked with a confident air and he was "extremely proud." Sam usually wore his hair braided and he smoked cigars.

When he ran away, Sam was wearing a homemade cotton shirt and pantaloons. He took a blue coat, a pair of boots, and other items with him when he ran away.

Campbell said Sam could be identified by the lash marks on his back and thighs that were made during the whippings his slaveholder had given him. Campbell claimed that Sam was "inclined to steal" and that he would soon provide himself with whatever he needed.

Campbell wanted Sam back because the slave was a good cook and an excellent waiter. Sam understood all kinds of farm work and the distilling business.

Campbell felt that Sam would try to get to Cincinnati and from there on to Canada.

Campbell offered a $10 reward and "reasonable" expenses to anyone who captured Sam within 60 miles of Nashville, and $20 if Sam were apprehended more than 60 miles away.

Source: *The Nashville Whig*, June 1, 1813.

June 22, 1813. A slave named Jeffery ran away from Doctor John Shelby's plantation in Gallatin, Tennessee. Jeffery was about six feet tall, and he spoke boldly.

Shelby offered a $30 reward if Jeffery was detained outside Tennessee and $20 if the runaway was captured within the state. As was usual in such instances, the slaveholder promised to pay "reasonable charges" if the slave was returned to him.

Source: *The Nashville Whig*, June 29, 1813.

Note: Dr John Shelby (1785-1859) joined General Andrew Jackson and took part in the Creek War. Shelby later served at the Battle of New Orleans. He gained fame as being perhaps America's greatest surgeon during that period.

July 3, 1813. George W. Sanders of Big Bone Cave in White County (now Van Buren County), Tennessee reported that a slave had escaped. The slave, named Jesse, was 27 or 28, and had once been held by a Dr. Ward. Jesse could be easily identified. Half his right ear had been "cut off" and he had a large scar on his left cheek.

Sanders offered $20 to anyone "who will apprehend [Sam] and secure him, so that I get him again."

Source: *The Nashville Whig*, August 24, 1813.

July 24, 1813. Frederick Stump (the father of the previously mentioned John Stump) of Whites Creek had lost a slave. But the slave named Ned wasn't a runaway; he had been stolen.

Ned was a good shoemaker. He was about 27, and he stood about six feet tall. He was stoutly built, but he walked with a limp. He had a visible scar on his face. When spoken to, he always responded with a smile.

Ned left atop a sorrel horse that stood about 15 hands high. The thin horse was six to eight years old.

Stump accused John D. Johnson (also known as John Drennings and John Lake) of stealing Ned and the horse. Johnson was about 30, he was heavyset, and he had a scar on his chin. One of his fingers had been broken which caused it to be gnarled, and he was missing the second toe on his left foot. Johnson was armed with a "well-fixed" rifle with a piece of silver on the barrel bearing the name of J. Young. Johnson was also believed to be carrying pistols.

Stump offered the hefty sum of $150 if Ned and the horse were returned, and Johnson was captured. He would pay $75 if Ned and the horse were returned, but Johnson got away. If Johnson were arrested, but Ned and the horse were not recovered, Stump would pay $100.

Source: *The Nashville Whig*, August 24, 1813.

August 19, 1813. A big two-day auction began to settle the estate of the late Meshach Haile. The auction took place on the Haile farm on Whites Creek about eight miles northwest of Nashville along the road to Clarksville. Sale items included seven horses, 16 cows, about 30 hogs, 10 sheep, five featherbeds, household furnishings, a wagon with gear, and a selection of farming implements. Added to that were 25 acres of standing corn and four slaves.

The slaves, two little boys and their mothers, were sold on August 20.

Source: *The Nashville Whig*, August 3, 1813.

August 20, 1813. G. G. Washington of Davidson County was selling three adult slaves and several juveniles. All the slaves were male. As payment, Washington was willing to accept negotiable notes redeemable at the Nashville bank.

Source: *The Nashville Whig*, January 1, 1813.

September 13, 1813. Thomas Blackney of Montgomery County petitioned the Tennessee legislature to allow him to emancipate a slave woman named Harriet. He also requested that her sons, Frederick, John, and Tobias be given the name Blackney and that they be emancipated as soon as they were of legal age.

Source: Office of Tennessee Secretary of State, *Tennessee Legislative Petitions*.

October 1, 1813. Thomas Eastland of The Stone Fort in Franklin County (now Coffee County), Tennessee offered a reward for the return of a runaway slave named Anthony.

Anthony was short. He was last seen wearing a blue coat and a large white hat.

Eastland believed that Anthony, who was "uncommonly artful," was either in the Nashville area or that he was trying to make his way back to his birth state of North Carolina.

Eastland offered a $10 reward if Anthony was captured in Tennessee and $20 if the slave was caught outside the state.

Anthony was captured before he made it to North Carolina, and he was returned to Eastland. However, he soon escaped again and tried to make it to Indian territory, but he was recaptured and returned again.

Unwilling to remain enslaved, on May 22, 1814, Anthony ran away for the third time. Eastland expected Anthony to resume his efforts to get to North Carolina or Indian Territory again.

When he made his third escape, Anthony was wearing a blue coat and pantaloons made from deer hides.

Eastland believed that Anthony might be using a pass given to him by a white man. Or the runaway slave might be able to spin a "plausible tale" in an attempt to prove he was a free man.

Eastland also cautioned that Anthony was dangerous because he would fight to keep from being captured.

Eastland offered a "generous reward" for Anthony's capture.

Sources: *The Nashville Whig*, October 12, 1813; *The Nashville Whig*, October May 22, 1814.

1814

January 3, 1814. A slave named Jerry ran away from Oliver Johnston's plantation at Lower Ferry near Nashville. Jerry had a light complexion, he was about 30, and he stood about 5'10". Jerry was stoop-shouldered, had a front tooth missing, and looked down as he walked along.

When he left, Jerry was carrying a large amount of clothing and was wearing a new coat. He also had $80 in his possession. Jerry was believed to be riding an old sorrel horse fourteen or fifteen hands high, but he would likely change it for a better one.

Although didn't have a pass, Jerry could probably move along easily by pretending to be a free man, especially since he had spending money. Johnston had recently purchased Jerry from Alex McDowell. McDowell had often sent Jerry to Kentucky with a cart to pick up paper. At those times, Jerry "was in the habit" of passing himself off as a free man.

McDowell had purchased Jerry from Joseph Johns and Jerry was believed to be traveling under the name of Jerry Johns. Jerry was considered dangerous because he was armed with a pistol and perhaps other weapons.

Johnston offered a reward of $20 for Jerry if he was captured within Tennessee and $30 if he was captured elsewhere.

Source: *The Nashville Whig*, January 4, 1814.

January 18, 1814. T. Overton lived about one-half mile from Saunders Ferry near Hendersonville, in Sumner County. Overton was looking to hire several slaves for the full year. He was especially in need of a blacksmith and a stonemason. He also wished to "lease 100 acres of good land, with a ferry and a boat on the Cumberland River."

Additionally, Overton was selling several hundred barrels of Indian corn and 30 to 40 tons of Timothy hay.

Source: *The Nashville Whig*, January 25, 1814.

January 29, 1814. Joseph Woods of Nashville had several items for sale including four kegs of rum, 2,000 pounds of logwood, 25 pounds of verdigris, one barrel of allspice, 100 pounds of copperas, one box of indigo, 400 pounds of sein twine, 500 yards of bagging, 150 buffalo robes, and three keel boats.

Woods also had a slave woman he wanted to hire out. She was a good cook, laundress, and spinner. Woods desired the slave woman to be placed in a home in the country.

Source: *The Nashville Whig*, March 8, 1814.

Note: Verdigris is a green or greenish-blue poisonous pigment

Note: Copperas are green crystals made from hydrated ferrous sulfate.

February 14, 1814. Alpha Kingsley was a Nashville real estate agent. He was selling several plantations in Davidson County. Additionally, he was selling several slaves, a pair of horses, and an "elegant" small coach.

Kingsley said he would accept one-third payment in cash, and the balance in negotiable notes secured by the Nashville Bank.

Source: *The Nashville Whig*, February 22, 1814.

March 8, 1814. David Craig lived six miles east of Franklin, Tennessee. He was offering a reward for a runaway slave named Moses. Moses was a youth, and he stood about 5'8".

Craig promised $10 to anyone who returned Moses to him or lodged the slave in a jail until retrieved.

Source: *The Nashville Whig*, March 8, 1814.

March 22, 1814. James G. Hicks wanted to purchase substantial amounts of lumber for his cabinet business. He also

had a number of slaves that he wanted to hire out. The slaves were men, women, and children. Some of them were good cooks.
Source: *The Nashville Whig*, February 22, 1814.

March 25, 1814. W. Tannehill & Company was selling a large assortment of blankets, clothing, and cloth. The company would take a slave boy and a horse as partial payment for its products.
Source: *The Nashville Whig*, March 23, 1814.

April 17, 1814. A slave named Celia was stolen from the Rutherford County plantation of Issac Shelby. Celia was 15 and she was "rather tall." She had light skin, a snubbed nose, gray eyes, and straight, light colored hair. Celia wasn't well spoken.

Celia could be identified by the scars on her arms made during the lashings she had received from her slaveholder.

When she was taken, Celia had several nice frocks, a pair of red slippers, and a bonnet with her.

Shelby offered $20 for Celia's return and another $30 for the arrest and conviction of the person that took her.
Source: *The Nashville Whig*, April 17, 1814.

Note: Slave women didn't escape from plantations as often as male slaves did, but women ran away more than is generally realized.

April 18, 1814. Davidson County jailer, E. Benoit, reported that he had a runaway slave named Peter in custody. Peter said he had escaped from the Ruben Westmoreland plantation in Davidson County.

Benoit requested that Westmoreland, or whoever held title to Peter to come forward, pay the jail fees, and take Peter away. Otherwise, according to the law, Benoit would sell Peter to pay the jail fees.
Source: *The Nashville Whig*, May 10, 1814.

April 20, 1814. John Garner had a slave girl of 15 or 16 for sale. He wanted cash or a negotiable note for her.
Source: *The Nashville Whig*, April 20, 1814.

April 26, 1814. William Gillispie lived in Sumner County about five miles from Gallatin. Gillispie said a slave named Derry had run away. Derry had a light complexion, was about 25, stood about 5'9", and had a few white hairs on the top of his head. Derry had a large scar on one of his arms that was caused by a burn he received as a child. He had a "down" look when spoken to.

Gillispie believed that Derry was using a pass given to him by a person living nearby. He also believed that Derry would try to get to Virginia or Ohio.

Gillispie was offering a $20 reward for Derry's return.
Source: *The Nashville Whig*, April 27, 1814.

April 30, 1814. Archer Cheatham of Springfield, Tennessee stated that a slave named Lewis had run off. Lewis was about 35 and he stood about 5'7". Lewis was "full-faced," light complexioned, stoutly built and bow legged. He could be identified by a large scar on one of his big toes. Cheatham said Lewis was talented, being a good cooper, shoe maker, and carpenter.

Cheatham purchased Lewis in North Carolina and he believed that Lewis might try to return there. He was offering $20 for the return of the runaway slave.
Source: *The Nashville Whig*, June 21, 1814.

Note: A cooper is a person who makes and repairs barrels, casks, and other types of wooden containers.

May 3, 1814. Samuel Bell lived on Mill Creek in Davidson County. He wanted to purchase a slave girl at least seven-years-old, but younger than 10. Bell was offering to pay in cash for the slave.
Source: *The Nashville Whig*, May 3, 1814.

May 6, 1814. The estate of Ann Hay was auctioned off. Items sold included one slave, horses, cattle, sheep, hogs, a yoke of oxen, a water dray, farming tools, whiskey, beer, a brew kettle, furniture, and bacon. Purchasers had nine months to pay.

Source: *The Nashville Whig*, May 3, 1814.

May 6, 1814. The estate of the late John Beck was auctioned off. Items sold included work horses, cattle, sheep, hogs, a still with tubs, bacon, corn, furniture, and plantation tools.

Additionally, some of the slaves Beck had held was put to auction. The estate administrators did sell his other slaves.

Source: *The Nashville Whig*, May 3, 1814.

May 20, 1814. With the Creek War concluded, General Andrew Jackson ordered his quartermaster to collect all monies due from the Creeks. He also ordered all slaves captured from Bob Cataulle sold "without delay." The money collected was earmarked for the widows and orphans of the soldiers of Jackson's command killed during the campaign against the Creeks.

Source: *The Nashville Whig*, June 7, 1814.

May 24, 1814. Captain Henry G. Gist reported that Washington Woody had deserted from the Army after accepting a signing bonus. Woody was well-known in southern Kentucky as an "awful specious fellow." He was also active in criminal enterprises in Tennessee. He operated between Gallatin and Knoxville stealing slaves, taking them to Kentucky, and then selling them.

Source: *The Nashville Whig*, August 2, 1814.

June 1, 1814. Montgomery Bell of Cumberland Furnace in Dickson County stated that a slave named Cary had run away. Cary was about 24, he stood about 5'9", and he was stoutly built. Bell purchased Cary from Rubin Pain of Dry Creek in 1813 and Cary had acquaintances in Nashville. Cary was, according to Bell, intelligent, but not honest or industrious.

Bell offered $20 for information regarding Cary leading to the slave's confinement or return.

As of July 2, 1816, more than two years after his escape, Cary was still free. On that day, Bell upped the reward for Cary to $300 and provided more information.

Bell related that Cary had changed his name to Buck and that he would change it again every time he moved to a new location. According to Bell, Cary had taken a keelboat southeast down the Cumberland River to Nashville. There, he signed on as a workman on the barge piloted by Captain Blackman headed to Cincinnati. However, Cary left the barge at Louisville and traveled northeast on foot with a man who lived at Brownsville, Pennsylvania. Cary stopped at Chillicothe, Ohio and stayed there for a while. Bell believed Cary had gotten hold of a forged pass at Chillicothe which allowed him to hire himself out after telling employers that he was on his way home. From Chillicothe, so believed Bell, Cary had traveled either to somewhere else in Ohio, or he gone on to Pittsburgh, or another Pennsylvania town.

Bell cautioned that Cary would never acknowledge that he was a fugitive slave and unless he was chained and closely guarded, he would escape.

Source: *The Nashville Whig*, August 9, 1814.

Note: Not all slaves were used in agricultural work. Some toiled in other industries and factories. The jobs they performed were often hot, dangerous, and labor intensive.

Note: Montgomery Bell (1769-1855) at one time held more slaves than any other person in Tennessee. He used slaves in his iron business and he helped make Tennessee the third-highest iron-producing state in the United States.

Along with his business ventures, he founded Montgomery Bell Academy and Montgomery Bell State Park.

June 6, 1814. John Garner wanted to purchase 500 bushels of corn. He also had a slave girl for sale. She was about 15 or 16-years-old.

Source: *The Nashville Whig*, May 3, 1814.

July 14, 1814. A Nashville slaveholder had several slave women who were "well acquainted with washing ironing and cooking." He was willing to sell them or hire them out by the month or the year.

Source: *The Nashville Whig*, August 2, 1814.

July 26, 1814. A slave holder in Nashville was selling three slaves. He had an "active fellow" who was 21 or 22. The young man was brought up to be a house servant, but he had done outside work for the past five or six years.

Another slave for sale was a young woman of about 20. She had been used mainly for outside labor, but she could do housework as well.

The third slave for sale was a woman of about 25. She could do field work as well as any man and could also handle household chores.

The seller was willing to accept credit if the purchaser could make bond and provide adequate security.

Source: *The Nashville Whig*, July 26, 1814.

August 1, 1814. Thomas Overton of Davidson County was offering $10 to anyone returning a slave named Tom to him. Tom was about 45. He had small eyes, and he was tall and slim. When spoken to, Tom always smiled and "answered without hesitation." Overton said Tom was an "awful sensible fellow."

Tom had been previously possessed by Robert Harrison of Virginia, but Overton didn't believe the runaway slave had gone there. Overton believed that Tom was being harbored by one of his neighbors.

Tom had left most of his clothes at the home of a man named Horne and had promised to return for them. Since then, Horne's wife had reported seeing Tom several times.

Source: *The Nashville Whig*, August 9, 1814.

August 15, 1814. John Harrod of Huntsville, Alabama Territory thought the slave named Charles was in Tennessee. Charles, a native born African, was 22 and he was a blacksmith by trade. He spoke English well, stood about 5'3", and he was strong. Charles was light complexioned and his face was pockmarked. He had "filed teeth" and the thumbs on both his hands were remarkably short.

Harrod claimed that Charles had been stolen by David May. May had once been whipped and branded in Franklin, Tennessee for horse stealing. Harrod said he had trailed May to Campbell County, in upper east Tennessee, but found that the thief had departed there in January 1815. After that, Herrod had lost May's trail.

Herrod offered a $25 reward to anyone for information about the whereabouts of Charles.

Source: *The Nashville Whig*, August 30, 1814.

August 15, 1814. Thomas Williamson of Nashville had a piece of property in town that he wanted to sell or trade. He was willing to trade the property for land, or for a combination of land and slaves.

Source: *The Nashville Whig*, August 30, 1814.

September 6, 1814. W. Barrow had two pieces of land on the Cumberland River seven miles north of Nashville. One tract was 276 acres and had cabins on it. The other was 250 acres and had a two-story house on it. Barrow was willing to accept cash, cash bonds, or slaves as payment.

Source: *The Nashville Whig*, September 6, 1814.

September 20, 1814. Joseph Wingate, the Dickson County jailer, announced that he had a runaway slave in custody who wasn't fluent in English. As best he could tell, the slave was named Miles. Miles was 5'8", and he was skinny. He wore blue beads around his neck and when captured he was carrying a club-axe. Wingate thought it was possible that Miles had been chopping wood recently.

Wingate requested that the slaveholder come forward, prove that Miles was his, pay the prison fees, and take the slave away. Otherwise, Miles would be auctioned off to the highest bidder to pay the jail fees.

Source: *The Nashville Whig*, September 20, 1814.

September 27, 1814. Auctioneer D. Robertson sold several items on the Nashville Public Square. He accepted whiskey or cotton in exchange for most items, but he required cash for the slave woman and two slave children he auctioned off.

Source: *The Nashville Whig*, September 20, 1814.

September 28, 1814. Elisha Green, who lived Gallatin, said he had a slave that had run away from his plantation. The slave named Sam had a flat face. His left leg was shorter than his right and his left ankle was larger than his right. Sam's toes were turned in and he walked with a limp. Sam also had scar on one shin caused by inflammation.

It was believed that Sam was wounded, having been stabbed with a knife at about the same time he ran away.

Green wanted Sam back. He promised that anyone returning the slave would be "handsomely rewarded."

Source: *The Nashville Whig*, October 25, 1814.

October 8, 1814. John J. Zollicoffer was from Maury County and he lived about six miles south of Columbia. He let it be known that a slave woman named Letty had run off. Letty was about 27, and she was about average height, but she was slender. Letty was stooped forward slightly, yet she had a "handsome countenance" and was "quick spoken." Letty was about six months pregnant.

Zollicoffer believed that Letty was most likely being sheltered in the vicinity of Nashville. But it was possible, he thought, that she might be trying to get back to her birthplace at Rhea County, Tennessee. He offered a $10 reward for her return.

Source: *The Nashville Whig*, December 6, 1814.

Note: John J. Zollicoffer was the father of Felix Zollicoffer (1812-1862). Felix Zollicoffer served in the United States House of Representatives and was a General in the Confederate States Army. He was killed in combat at the Battle of Mill Springs (Kentucky) on January 19, 1862.

November 15, 1814. A slave named Charles ran away from the George Smith plantation near Nashville. Charles was a plasterer by trade. He was slender and had a light complexion. Charles had large "white eyes," and he spoke boldly and sensibly. His right foot was deformed causing him to limp. Smith believed the slave had gotten a pass in some way, and that he was using it.

Smith offered a $10 reward if Charles was captured in Tennessee, and $20 if the runaway was detained out of state.

Source: *The Nashville Whig*, January 3, 1815.

December 6, 1814. Eleven slaves ran away from the plantation owned by James Austin on Stones River in Davidson County.

The slaves were Charles, his wife, and their three children; a slave woman named Betty, and her three children; and a slave woman named Nancy, and her child.

Austin promised a "liberal reward" to anyone returning the runaways. However, he wanted them delivered to Silas Flournoy who lived about five miles north of Nashville.

Source: *The Nashville Whig*, December 13, 1814.

1815

January 8, 1815. John Haggatt had three young slave boys, and a slave woman for hire.
Source: *The Nashville Whig*, December 13, 1814.

January 10, 1815. A Nashvillian was looking for an overseer. The overseer's job would be to manage the slaves on the plantation and ensure its efficient operation. To that end, the overseer would enforce discipline and administer punishments to the slaves.
Source: *The Nashville Whig*, January 17, 1815.

Note: Overseers acted as foremen on plantations, and some big plantations had more than one overseer. While it was rare, sometimes free Black men were hired to be overseers.

January 12, 1815. Edward Ward, the executor of the Peter Jones estate, had several slaves for hire. They included "men, women, boys, and girls."

On December 30, 1815, Edward Ward sold the Sanders & Chandler cotton factory, which was a part of the General Chamberlain Jones estate, along with a number of horses. Additionally, Ward again leased the slaves (men, women, boys, and girls), for the year of 1816.

On January 11, 1817, Ward once again leased the slaves belonging to Jones.

On December 18, 1818, Edward Jones said the Peter Jones slaves were expected to be returned with all their clothes. They were leased again on December 26.

Edward Ward continued to hire out slaves for several years. On April 4, 1821, he announced that he would hire out slaves (men, women, boys, and girls) until November 1 of that year.

Sources: *The Nashville Whig*, January 17, 1815; Source: *The Nashville Whig*, January 11, 1817; *The Nashville Whig and Tennessee Advertiser*, December 19, 1818; *The Nashville Whig*, April 4, 1821.

February 28, 1815. David Sutton wanted to trade a few of his slaves for cotton. He had "a young fellow, a girl, or a boy" available for trade.

Source: *The Nashville Whig*, February 28, 1815.

February 28, 1815. A man living at the Nashville Inn had five young male slaves for sale.

Source: *The Nashville Whig*, January 17, 1815.

Note: The Nashville Inn was established in 1796. Over the next 60 years it hosted many famous people. Governor, and future President, Andrew Johnson was living there when the hotel burned down in 1856.

March 8, 1815. Nancy Parham, the executrix of the William Perham estate, sold his property located near Thomas Talbot's farm in Davidson County. At the same time, she hired out the male slaves he had held title to for a term running until December 25.

Source: *The Nashville Whig*, February 28, 1815.

March 28, 1815. A Nashvillian wanted to purchase a "smart active" slave boy between the ages of 12 and 16. He promised to pay a "liberal price" for just the right slave.

Source: *The Nashville Whig*, January 17, 1815.

May 15, 1815. A slave named Randolph escaped from Thomas Washington's plantation in Rutherford County. Randolph was 22, light complexioned, he stood about 5'9", was stoutly built, and he was "apt" to stutter. Randolph was also knock-kneed, and he walked with a quick gait.

Source: *The Nashville Whig*, October 10, 1815.

May 30, 1815. John P. Brodnax had 143 acres of land (40 of which were cleared) for sale in Franklin, Tennessee. He was willing to take cash or slaves for the property.

Source: *The Nashville Whig*, May 30, 1815.

June 6, 1815. Charles Harvey was attempting to sell 11 slaves in Tennessee. He claimed he had the right to do so because he had received a power of attorney a man named James Harvey Sr. Harvey lived in Louisburg, North Carolina. The slaves for sale included:

Gilbert, who was about 30. He was a good blacksmith.

Gilbert's wife Polly. Harvey Sr. purchased Elisha from a man named Williams who lived in Davidson County.

Polly's four children, Lucy, Peggy, Jack, and a small child.

Cyrus, who was "a little lame" in one hip.

China and her children, Rebecca, Alfred, and Eliza.

The partners of James Harvey, Sr. claimed that he had no ability to give a power of attorney to Charles Harvey. They said the long-standing co-partnership agreement between James Harvey Sr., Allen Harvey, and James Harvey Jr. was still in force, and the agreement precluded the power of attorney, and that the power of attorney was void.

The other partners claimed their "right & share" to the 11 slaves. They promised to retrieve the slaves sold by Charles Harvey.

On July 24, James Harvey Sr. answered the charge that he had no power to grant the power of attorney to sell the slaves. Harvey Sr. claimed those accusing him were engaging in a "gross, palpable, and diabolical falsehood." Moreover, he called their claims "wicked and nefarious." He continued that his accusers "never had any right or claim to any portion" of his property.

Harvey Sr. finished by saying that "Charles Harvey is authorized by power of attorney, duly executed and legally authenticated, to sell all or any part of my property in the state of Tennessee, for the purpose of meeting the claims of my just creditors – the sales therefore that he may make, and the titles he may execute, will be good and valid to all intents and purposes."

Sources: *The Nashville Whig*, June 13, 1815; Source: *The Nashville Whig*, July 15, 1815.

June 26, 1815. A Nashvillian was in the market for a slave boy of between 10 and 12 years old. He didn't specify exactly what type of work he intended the slave boy to do.

Source: *The Nashville Whig*, July 4, 1815.

July 16, 1815. A slave named Jack escaped from the William McDonald plantation. Jack was about 21-years-old, and he stood about 5'10". Jack laughed and showed his teeth when spoken to. His second toe on each foot was larger than his "big" toe.

When he ran away, Jack had on an old fur hat, a homespun coatee, and chambray pantaloons. Jack had other garments with him which led McDonald to believe that the slave may have changed clothes.

McDonald expected Jack to head for the Duck River area, because he knew people there. He offered $5 to anyone that found and captured Jack in Tennessee and $10 if he were captured elsewhere.

Source: *The Nashville Whig*, July 25, 1815.

Note: A coatee was a type of tight-fitting coat or jacket which was waist length at the front and had short tails behind. It was worn by soldiers and civilians alike.

Note: Chambray is a type of fabric made from either linen or cotton.

July 21, 1815. Two slaves (Frank and Billy) escaped from Andrew Barnett's plantation and he thought they were headed for the Nashville area.

Frank was 22, thin, and he stood about 5'6". He had a small scar which went from his nose to his left cheek. Frank was smart and he could read very well.

Barnett said he had marked Frank by filing "several notches between several of his upper fore teeth." The notches were "very plain." About a year earlier, Barnett had also branded Frank on each cheek with the letter "B." But the brands were "not very perceivable."

Billy was about 18, was heavyset, and he stood about 5'9". Part of one of his ears had been bitten off, and he had a black speck about the size of a pea in the white of one of his eyes.

Barnett offered a reward of between $20 and $50 for the return of the two slaves.

Source: *The Nashville Whig*, August 8, 1815.

August 7, 1815. A slave named Solomon ran away from the William Rutherford plantation about four miles from Nashville. Solomon was 22, and he stood about 5'10".

At the time of his escape Solomon was wearing a blue linsey coat with yellow metal buttons, an old fur hat which had been repaired, and an old yellow waistcoat. When Solomon ran off, he took a buffalo robe, two or three pairs of homespun pantaloons, and several other articles of clothing.

Rutherford believed it probable that Solomon would try to obtain a pass and use it to help him get to North Carolina. Rutherford offered a $20 reward if Solomon was captured in Tennessee, and $40 if he was captured elsewhere.

Source: *The Nashville Whig*, August 15, 1815.

Note: Linsey (often called linsey-woolsey) is a coarse, twill or plain-woven fabric traditionally made with a linen warp (vertical threads) and a wool weft (horizontal threads).

Note: A waistcoat was a close-fitting, sleeveless garment worn by men under a suit jacket or coat.

August 10, 1815. General Andrew Jackson gained national fame in January 1815 with his victory at the Battle of New Orleans. That victory eventually propelled Jackson to the presidency. However, immediately after the war, he returned to his plantation in Nashville that would come to be called the Hermitage.

Jackson reported that a slave named Ned escaped from his plantation. Ned was 25, light complexioned, and he stood about 5'8". He had a long face and was "very sprightly." He had proven himself to be a good cook and "body servant."

When Ned ran away, he was wearing a blue broad-cloth coat, pantaloons, a straw hat, and affair-top boots. He also took a pair of saddlebags, and clothing into which he had probably changed.

Ned had reportedly been seen "loitering" around the Nashville Inn where he had worked for four or five years. However, he hadn't been sighted there for some time. Jackson felt Ned had either left the area or had "been taken off by some villain."

Jackson offered a $25 reward if Ned was captured in state, or $50 if he was captured elsewhere. However, Jackson cautioned that Ned was crafty enough to get away from captors, "unless well-secured."

Source: *The Nashville Whig*, September 15, 1815.

Note: Affair-top boots were boots that had the distinctive feature of a contrasting colored "top" created by folding down the boot shaft.

August 18, 1815. A 36-year-old slave named Amia escaped from William Donelson's plantation near Dry Creek in Davidson County. Amia was a large woman. She had a round face and full eyes. Amia had a noticeable scar on the back of her head near the hair line.

Donelson believed Amia was "enticed" to run away by an escaped slave named Bristol. About six months before, named

Bristol had escaped from the plantation of Thomas Napier located near the Yellow Creek Iron Works in Montgomery County. Bristol was thin and he was missing the middle finger of his right hand.

Donelson cautioned that Bristol was a "well-armed" and "very notorious runaway." Donelson continued that Bristol had "as bad a character" as any slave. Donelson contended that Bristol had been captured "once or twice" only to escape again.

Donelson offered $100 to anyone who could capture Amia and Bristol, or he would pay $50 for Amia alone.

Source: *The Nashville Whig*, August 18, 1815.

September 5, 1815. A Nashvillian had a young slave and her first child for sale. He was willing to trade them for a woman slave of between the ages of 20 to 25.

Source: *The Nashville Whig*, September 12, 1815.

September 12, 1815. Thomas Washington had another slave escape from his plantation. The above-mentioned Randolph (see May 15, 1815) had still not been captured when a slave named Soloman ran off.

Soloman was 28, and he stood about 5'10". He was bow-legged, had two upper front teeth missing, and had a scar on his right cheek. Solomon had a more distinctive feature, however. He had been born with six fingers on each hand. His first slave master had chopped the extra digits off, but the nubs were still visible.

Washington offered $10 each for the return of Randolph and Solomon if they were captured outside of Tennessee, and $5 each if taken within the state.

Source: *The Nashville Whig*, October 10, 1815.

September 18, 1815. A petition was delivered to the Tennessee legislature requesting that it pass a law abolishing slavery.

Source: Office of Tennessee Secretary of State, *Tennessee Legislative Petitions*.

November 18, 1815. The Warren County jailer in McMinnville, Merit Ware, had a slave lodged in his jail. Merit said the slave was about 28, had a light complexion, and stood about 5'10". He said the slave had confessed to escaping from Thomas Thompson's plantation in Davidson County.

Source: *The Nashville Whig*, December 5, 1815.

November 19, 1815. Dickson County jailer, Joseph Wingate, had another runaway slave lodged in his jail. The slave said his name was Andrew. He stood about 5'10", and he appeared to be between 45 and 50.

Andrew was wearing a long, pale blue homespun coat.

Andrew said he had been living on the plantation belonging to Christopher Hutchins in Bedford County when he escaped. Wingate requested that Hutchins come, pay the jail fees, and take Andrew away.

Source: *The Nashville Whig*, December 5, 1815.

November 20, 1815. Stokley Hays and Francis Sanders were business partners. They reported the escape of three slaves near Nashville. According to Hays and Sanders all three slaves, Sam, Nankana, and Luck, were born in Africa and brought to America aboard a slave ship.

Sam was about 25. He was tall and skinny and he spoke English fairly well.

Nankana was average size and about 30 years of age. He was light complexioned, his face bore an African tribal mark, and he had exceptionally long front teeth which appeared to be filed down, but he said they weren't. According to Nankana, his teeth were that way because of a fall from a tree. Nankana's English was poor and it was difficult for the slavers to communicate with him.

Luck was about 40-years-old and he was of average size.

The three slaves had been brought to Tennessee from Georgia during the summer of 1815 by Richard Tullus and Sam S. Starns. The presumption was that the slaves would travel together, and that they would try to get back to Augusta, Georgia.

The reward for the three was $10 each if found in Tennessee, and $20 each if they were found elsewhere.

Source: *The Nashville Whig*, November 28, 1815.

Note: African tribal marks were commonly found on slaves brought to the New World directly from Africa. The marks varied depending upon the group to which each individual belonged.

November 30, 1815. William Creel sold the Benjamin Severn estate about three miles east of Stones River. The estate consisted of more than 200 acres of land, 50 acres of which had been cleared. Also on the auction block were 100 barrels of corn, farm implements, and two young slaves (one boy and one girl). Buyers were granted a year to pay.

Source: *The Nashville Whig*, October 10, 1815.

December 5, 1815. Slaveholder John Chapman of Davidson County reported that a slave named Mingo had escaped. Mingo stood about 5'10". He was about 42, but he looked much older. The gray-haired slave suffered from a hernia and wore trusses.

Chapman had purchased Mingo from a man names Joseph Pitts in Robertson County, and Chapman thought was that Mingo might try to return there.

Considering Mingo's apparent lack of value as a laborer, Chapman was willing to pay a substantial amount to get the slave back. Chapman offered a reward of $5 if Mingo was found in Davidson County and returned to him. He would pay $10 if Mingo were found elsewhere in Tennessee, and $30 if Mingo were found outside of the state.

Source: *The Nashville Whig*, December 12, 1815.

December 5, 1815. A Nashvillian had a slave girl and her child for sale. The mother was 17, and the baby was 9 months old. The mother could do housework or toil in the fields, depending upon the needs of the purchaser.

Source: *The Nashville Whig*, December 5, 1815.

December 15, 1815. Kiddy Robertson, the administrator of the Jonathan F. Robertson estate, sold all his property except for the slaves he had held. The slaves were leased out.

Source: *The Nashville Whig*, December 5, 1815.

December 26, 1815. Haslep & Vanleer was a Pennsylvania company. It leased the Napier Forge and Furnace operation in Nashville. The company needed workers to operate the faculty, and it hired 50 slaves from area plantation owners. Haslep & Vanleer promised to be "responsible for the wages and treatment of the slaves."

Source: *The Nashville Whig*, December 26, 1815.

December 30, 1815. William Maxey, the administrator of the John Pride estate, organized an auction at the Nashville Courthouse where 13 slaves were sold. Most of the slaves were sold as field hands, but one was a shoe and boot cobbler who had his own tools, and another one was a good "house woman" with two children. Winning bidders with good collateral didn't have to pay until December 25, 1816.

Source: *The Nashville Whig*, December 12, 1815.

1816

January 16, 1816. Thomas J. Reid wanted to purchase a for a "sober, industrious" slave. He was offering to pay "a liberal price, in cash."

Source: *The Nashville Whig*, January 16, 1816.

January 20, 1816. A slave named Jack escaped from the plantation of Alex Porter. Jack was about 28, he stood about 5'10", wore a long beard, and spoke slowly.

Several slave masters had held Jack. A Mr. Probit of Buck, North Carolina first held Jack. John Wilson purchased Jack and brought him to Tennessee. John Wilson sold Jack to William Wilson who sold him to William Kidd, who sold him to Alex Porter.

When he was last seen, Jack was wearing an old, dark colored homespun coat, a pair of twilled gray overalls (the type worn by soldiers), a woolen hat, a cotton shirt, white woolen socks, and a pair of Brogan shoes.

A doctor had been treating Jack for venereal disease for some time. Porter thought Jack might try to buy medicine in Nashville.

Porter offered $20 for Jack's return.

Source: *The Nashville Whig*, January 23, 1816.

Note: Brogans are strong, ankle-high work shoes or boots that are designed to be used by laborers and to last for many years. They weren't made for comfort.

Note: The first effective treatment for venereal disease wasn't introduced until about 1910. Before then, the treatments often involved mercury, used in ointments, vapor baths, and douches.

These treatments often lead to mercury poisoning and kidney failure. Various herbs were used as treatments as well.

March 3, 1816. A slave named Major had once been held by Thomas Masterson, and when Masterson died, Baker Wrather claimed Major. Major, who was average size, worked on the Wrather plantation in Lebanon, Tennessee for a time, then he escaped.

When he ran away, Major took a small sorrel horse and a "good saddle with plated stirrup irons" with him.

Wrather thought Major was in Nashville. Major's wife was a slave toiling on Joseph Wood's plantation there and it was likely that Major may have been trying to get back to her.

Wrather also thought it possible that someone had persuaded Major to go with him, and that the unnamed thief was now concealing the slave. Wrather cautioned anyone against trading with or harboring Major and he promised to prosecute anyone who did so.

Wrather promised that if Major returned on his own, he would be forgiven. Wrather also promised that if Major came back, he would sell him to a Nashville slaveholder so Major could be near his wife.

Wrather offered a $5 reward to anyone turning Major over to the authorities, or $10 if Major was returned directly to him.

Source: *The Nashville Whig*, April 9, 1816.

March 19, 1816. William Maxey was in the market for three young slaves. He wanted to purchase two boys and one girl between the ages of 12 and 20.

Source: *The Nashville Whig*, March 19, 1816.

March 20, 1816. A slave named Frank escaped from the Giles Harding plantation on Richland Creek in Davidson County. Frank was 20 or 21, and he stood about six feet tall.

When Frank ran away, he was wearing a dark colored homespun coat, dark pantaloons, and a fur hat. He also took other cloths with him.

Frank had been brought to Tennessee from Virginia just a few weeks before, and Harding expected him to try to get back there. Harding offered a reward of $10 for Frank's return.

Frank was captured and returned sometime after April 16, but he escaped again on June 25. Harding again offered $10 for Frank's return.

Source: *The Nashville Whig*, April 2, 1816.

April 2, 1816. A slave named Sam escaped from Thomas Martin. Sam was about 27, he stood about 5'6", and he had one of his front teeth out. Sam was talented and he was fond of playing the banjo and dancing.

Sam was wearing a pair of copper-colored pantaloons, a homespun coat of mixed cloth, and a ruffled shirt when he ran away. However, he had several other changes of clothes with him.

Sam was last seen at Jesse Parker's plantation situated on Whites Creek. Sam's wife was a slave of Parker's. Martin believed Sam was still in the area.

Martin was offering $10 to anyone capturing Sam in Tennessee and twice as much if he was captured elsewhere.

Source: *The Nashville Whig*, April 9, 1816.

May 6, 1816. Edgar Hogan of Jackson County, Tennessee related that a slave named Gilbert had escaped. Gilbert was about 30 and he stood about six feet tall. He was a blacksmith by trade and had been a blacksmith in Nashville while enslaved there.

James Harvey of North Carolina had owned Gilbert. Hogan purchased Gilbert from Harvey through an attorney. Hogan was offering to pay $50 and expenses to get Gilbert back.

Source: *The Nashville Whig*, June 11, 1816.

May 8, 1816. Sumner County jailer, Jacob Seavea, imprisoned a slave named Lucy. Lucy was a stoutly built 20-year-old. She told

Seavea that she belonged to either Richard Nichols or to his daughter Peggy. Nichols and his daughter lived on the Duck River.

Seavea said either the father or daughter could pay the jail fees and take Lucy. Seavea also stated that if no one claimed Lucy, she would be sold for the accrued fees.

Source: *The Nashville Whig*, June 4, 1816.

May 14, 1816. James Vinson alerted the public that he owned the property Bethal Vinson was farming in Sumner County. James also claimed the title to the slave named Abram that Bethal was using to work the property. James warned that no one should purchase the property or Abram from Bethal.

Source: *The Nashville Whig*, May 21, 1816.

May 28, 1816. Stephen Cantrell & Company wanted to purchase several slaves. They wanted men, women, boys, and girls for which they would pay "liberal prices in cash."

Source: *The Nashville Whig*, June 11, 1816.

May 28, 1816. Robert Sample lived three miles east of Franklin, Tennessee. He had nine slaves for sale. Included was a 28-year-old man, his 25-year-old wife, and her seven children (three boys and four girls). The eldest child was about 11, and the youngest was an infant.

Source: *The Nashville Whig*, June 18, 1816.

June 1, 1816. The tax assessor for Tennessee's Fifth District at Williamson County sold 10 slaves for taxes owed. Included were two males under 12 years old; three males between 12 and 50; one male over 50; two females under 12; one female between 12 and 50; and one female over 50.

Source: *The Nashville Whig*, June 18, 1816.

June 20, 1816. Montgomery Bell reported that another slave had escaped from Cumberland Furnace. The slave was named

Bob and he was 22 or 23-years-old. He was about normal size and had corns covering the middle toes on both his feet.

When Bob ran away, he was wearing a coat made from mixed cloth. The coat had white basket buttons. However, Bell believed Bob would change clothes at his first opportunity.

Bell had purchased Bob from Major David Smith who lived on Elk Fork just off the Red River. Smith had purchased Bob from Frederick Hise of Russellville, Kentucky. Bell believed that Bob might try to get back to Russellville, but he felt it more likely that Bob would seek to go to Pittsburgh either as a part of a boat crew on the Ohio River, or on foot. This was because Bob had relations in Pittsburgh.

Bell didn't believe that Bob would ever concede that he was a fugitive slave and that if he weren't "securely ironed and taken care of," he would try to escape. Bell offered a $50 reward for Bob's return.

Source: *The Nashville Whig*, July 2, 1816.

Note: A basket button was usually put on coats. They were often made of silk fashioned over a pasteboard mold, which has a basket weave design.

July 4, 1816. A slave named Richard Numan escaped from the James Lewis plantation in Franklin County near Winchester, Tennessee. Richard was 21, slightly larger than normal, and muscular.

Richard ran way wearing a roundabout, and brown velvet pantaloons. He was a good blacksmith, harness maker, and shoemaker. Richard was also an excellent carriage and wagon driver, and a good barber.

Richard was highly intelligent, and Lewis believed the runaway would try to obtain a pass.

In other times, Richard had been a waiter and he was known in Virginia, Kentucky, and Tennessee.

Lewis offered a reward of $50 if Richard was captured out of state, $25 if he was detained in Tennessee, and $10 if he was caught in Franklin County.

Source: *The Nashville Whig*, July 16, 1816.

Note: A roundabout was a short, close-fitting jacket or coat made for men and boys. But sometimes, slave women wore them as well.

July 8, 1816. Elizabeth Stone, Bartholomew Stone, and William Stone Jr., executors of the estate of William Stone Sr., sold the elder Stone's slaves at the Dickson County Courthouse in Charolette, Tennessee.

Source: *The Nashville Whig*, July 2, 1816.

July 15, 1816. A slave named Michael escaped from the plantation owned by John Hughes at Woodville (in present-day Coffee County, Tennessee, southwest of Nashville). Michael was about 28. He had a light complexion, and his front teeth were gapped. Hughes purchased Michael from a man named William Lackie, but Michael had been bought and sold several times before.

After a previous runaway event in 1815, Michael had been lodged in the jail in Washington County, Tennessee. He escaped during a jail break and was at large before his recapture. While in the Washington County lockup, Michael told another prisoner that he had been in Nashville. Hughes believed that Michael would try to get back there.

Hughes offered a $50 reward for Michael regardless of where he was captured.

Source: *The Nashville Whig*, April 30, 1817.

August 26, 1816. A slave named William escaped from the plantation owned by William Crawford. The plantation was on the west fork of Station Camp Creek in Sumner County. William was about 25, he had a light complexion, was short and heavy, and had "large whiskers."

Crawford's belief that William was still "lurking" around the Nashville area was confirmed on August 28, when someone spotted William on the plantation owned by John Nichols.

Crawford offered $10 for William's return.

Source: *The Nashville Whig*, September 3, 1816.

September 10, 1816. A slave woman named Sally escaped from the Nashville Inn where she was working. Sally was 25, had long, straight hair, and she was highly intelligent.

Clayton Talbot claimed title to Sally and he had leased her to the hotel. When Talbot came to Nashville, Sally feared that he would take her to Huntsville, Alabama Territory with him and she spirited away immediately.

Talbot offered $25 for Sally's return.

Source: *The Nashville Whig*, September 24, 1816.

October 1, 1816. A slave named Solomon escaped from the plantation near Nashville owned by John B. Craighead. Solomon was 5'9". He was strong, and he "stooped forward a little," He was "very artful."

When he ran away, Solomon was wearing a pair of old nankeen pantaloons, a shirt, and an old British Army uniform coat.

Craighead believed that Solomon was trying to get to the lead mines in Missouri Territory. Craighead offered $25 if Solomon was arrested in Tennessee, or $50 if the runaway was returned from out of state.

Source: *The Nashville Whig*, October 29, 1816.

Note: The Missouri Lead Mines were in the Southeast Missouri Lead District (also known as the Old Lead Belt). They were once a one of the most important lead production operations in the world.

Note: Nankeen is a pale-yellow cloth made from a variety of cotton originally grown China.

November 12, 1816. Susan Anthony, administrator of the W. B. Anthony estate, had several slaves at Madison's Creek in Sumner County for hire. She wanted them hired out before the first of the new year, and she required "bond and approved security."

On December 8, 1817, Anthony announced that she was hiring out her slaves again. She said one of them was an unmarried "valuable house woman."

Near the end of 1818, Anthony again hired out the slaves. She said she had an excellent collier, a good wagoner, and seven plantation hands "of first-rate character." Additionally, she had other men and boys, and one or two slave girls between the ages of 13 and 16.

As she had in past years, Anthony was hiring slaves for the 1821 calendar year. On November 29, 1820, she announced that she had men, women, boys, and girls for hire. One of the men was a first-rate cook, and a house servant. Several of the men were first-rate plantation hands, while others were outstanding waggoneers. One of the women was a good cook, washer woman, and ironer.

Sources: *The Nashville Whig*, November 19, 1816; *The Nashville Whig*, December 8, 1817; *The Nashville Whig and Tennessee Advertiser*, November 14, 1818; *The Nashville Whig*, November 29, 1820.

November 19, 1816. At midday, between 30 and 40 slaves (men, women, boys, and girls) previously held by the late William Wharton were auctioned off at the Davidson County Courthouse in Nashville. The sellers said that based on both "their good qualities and appearances," they were the best slaves ever put on sale in the city.

The sellers only desired bidders who wanted to use the slaves for their own purposes. They didn't want speculators to bid on them. The sellers were offering one year of credit, with interest being charged after six months.

Source: *The Nashville Whig*, October 29, 1816.

November 21, 1816. Wilson County Sheriff Thomas Bradley distributed the information that he had impounded a slave named Reuben in the jail at Lebanon. Reuben told the Sheriff that Montgomery Bell owned him.

Bradley requested that Bell "come forward, claim his property, and pay" the jail charges. Otherwise, Bradley would sell Reuben to pay the jail expenses.

Source: *The Nashville Whig*, November 26, 1816.

December 17, 1816. Robert Searcy, Stephen Cantrell, and J. Wharton, executors of the George M. Deaderick estate, sold the property on Browns Creek in Davidson County. Along with real estate and Deaderick's personal belongings, they sold several slaves.

Source: *The Nashville Whig*, November 26, 1816.

December 25, 1816. James Russell of Summer Street in Nashville had seven slaves for sale. He had both male and female slaves and they ranged in age from 13 to 25. Russell, who said he was selling the slaves because he needed to raise funds, was willing to take cash, or he would accept short-term credit.

Source: *The Nashville Whig*, December 25, 1816.

1817

January 28, 1817. Davidson County jailer Samuel McChesney announced that he had placed a slave named Dick in jail. Dick was about 28, and he stood about 5'9". Dick told the jailer that Elizabeth McCullough of Davidson County owned him.

The jailer requested that McCullough come to the jail, pay the jail fee, and take Dick away.

Source: *The Nashville Whig*, February 19, 1817.

February 19, 1817. Thomas Dillahunty of Richland Creek in Davidson County wanted to purchase three or four slaves under the age of 15. He was offering to pay "a generous price in cash" for them.

By the first of December Dillahunty had sold his real estate in preparation for his move to Alabama Territory.

Additionally, he was in the market for two more young slaves between the ages of 15 and 20. Dillahunty offered prospective sellers an incentive. He said he was willing to pay for the slaves in silver.

Source: *The Nashville Whig*, February 26, 1817.

March 1, 1817. Thomas W. Easley, the Hickman County jailer, placed three slaves in his jail at the town of Vernon, Tennessee.

One of the slaves was named Calloway. He was about 30, and he stood about 5'10".

Additionally, there was a woman of about 25, and her child of about two and a half.

The slaves were captured with two horses, one a sorel and the other a bay. They also had old clothes with them and they were in possession of a pass.

The adult slaves said they belonged to a man named Stephens who purchased them from William Bissel. Both Stephens and Bissel lived in Williamson County, Tennessee.

Easley requested that Stephens, or any other person with title to the three slaves, come for them.

Source: *The Nashville Whig*, March 19, 1817.

March 1, 1817. The Robertson & Curry Auction Company held a sale at the Courthouse in Nashville. They sold the Elk Tavern which was located on College Street. The sellers offered one or two years of credit or they would accept young slaves "at cash value," provided the slaves were delivered at least 60 days before the debt came due.

Source: *The Nashville Whig*, February 12, 1817.

March 12, 1817. Pleasant Craddock had two slaves, a woman and a child, for sale. The woman had been consigned to the child, but she was not the child's mother.

Source: *The Nashville Whig*, March 12, 1817.

March 25, 1817. Because Joel Childress was moving to another plantation, he sold his properties in and near Murfreesboro, except for his store. He put a dwelling adjacent to the town square and two plantations on the auction block. One plantation was called "Handsome View" and the other "Race Turf." Childress was willing to take cash or slaves for the properties.

Source: *The Nashville Whig*, February 19, 1817.

April 2, 1817. E. Baker who resided at the Bell Tavern wanted a man slave who was suitable to be a personal servant. Additionally, he wanted to purchase two boy slaves.

Source: *The Nashville Whig*, April 9, 1817.

April 16, 1817. James Brown was the agent for the Nashville Steam Mill. He was looking to rent 10 or 12 slaves to work there. Brown asked the citizens of Nashville and its vicinity to direct those with slaves for hire his way as quickly as possible. He said it was "essential" to get the "mill in operation to meet the next crop."

Source: *The Nashville Whig*, April 16, 1817.

April 30, 1817. A slave named Bob escaped from a Nashville plantation owned by Roger B. Sappington. Bob, who was owned by Matthias B. Murphree, was about 27. He was slender, and he stood about 5'10".

Sappington had given Bob a pass allowing him to go to Major Dunn's plantation on Mansker's Creek. However, instead of going there, Bob ran away.

Murphree offered a $50 reward if Bob was captured outside of Tennessee and returned, and $30 if he was returned from inside the state.

Source: *The Nashville Whig*, April 30, 1817.

April 30, 1817. Thomas Easley had another runaway slave in the Hickman County jail. The slave was named Joe. He was about 19, and he stood just over 5'6". Joe said he belonged to Edward Cox of Double Springs, Alabama Territory near Fort Deposit.

Joe said he was "seduced away by James Roberts, under a promise of Freedom."

Easley made the usual request for the person with the legal claim to the slave to come forward, pay the jail fee, and take him away.

Source: *The Nashville Whig*, April 30, 1817.

May 4, 1817. Cylon Harris was six-years-old. His parents were an interracial couple. He lived with his grandfather, Gibson Harris, about seven miles west of Knoxville. The child was about 3' 7". He had a dark complexion and he was "very smart for his age."

A kidnapper, perhaps with an accomplice, abducted Cylon from his grandfather's home. Gibson described the kidnapper as a "large red-faced man, black hair, small black whiskers, and (it is believed) blue eyes."

The kidnapper was wearing black velvet pantaloons, a pale blue cotton or mixed cloth coat, and a hat with a large brim.

Gibson believed that even though the child was free, the kidnapper intended to sell him into slavery. To prevent that, Gibson offered $100 for his grandson's safe return.

Source: *The Nashville Whig*, May 19, 1817.

July 3, 1817. David Marshall of Lebanon reported that two of his slaves had been stolen. The slaves, two sisters, were named Minta and Nancy.

Minta was 18. She was "well-formed," and walked "with her toes pretty much turned out." Minta had an "open, frank countenance."

Nancy was 16. She was similar in manners to her sister. However, Nancy was shorter than average. She was also nearly bald and because of it, she usually wore a bonnet.

Marshall had purchased the sisters from Henry G. Kearney of Maury County on November 16. Kearney had gotten them from William Word of Wilson County.

Marshall offered a $25 reward each for the sisters and $100 for the thief.

Source: *The Nashville Whig*, July 21, 1817.

July 21, 1817. Samuel Hermann was willing to pay cash for several slaves between the ages of 14 and 18. He was especially in the market for slaves who were tradesmen such as barrel makers, blacksmiths, and brick masons. Additionally, he was interested in purchasing entire slave families.

Source: *The Nashville Whig*, July 21, 1817.

July 24, 1817. The Nashville City Aldermen passed an ordinance designed to stop the spread of smallpox in the city. All people, including slaves, with smallpox were required to vacate Nashville.

There was a $50 fine imposed for every infected person who was not removed from the city.

Source: *The Nashville Whig and Tennessee Advertiser*, May 30, 1818.

August 29, 1817. Davidson County jailer Samuel McChesney reported that he had taken a slave into custody. The runaway was between 18 and 20 years of age, and he stood about 5'5".

The slave claimed to belong to a man named Isaac Holden who lived near Fayetteville.

McChesney requested that Harden come to the jail and get the slave.

Source: *The Nashville Whig*, September 1, 1817.

August 30, 1817. Jason Thompson, who owned a plantation south of Nashville, reported an escaped slave. The runaway was a woman named Mary. Mary was pregnant. She stood about 5'4", and she had a visible scar on the left side of her neck.

When Mary left, she had an old, blue bombazine frock, but she wasn't wearing a hat or shoes.

Thompson expected Mary to attempt to reach either Lexington, Kentucky or Charlotte, Virginia. He offered a $5 reward if Mary was found in Davidson County and returned, $10 if found elsewhere in Tennessee, or $20 if she was captured outside the state.

Source: *The Nashville Whig*, September 8, 1817.

Note: Bombazine (sometimes called, bombasine) was fabric originally made of silk, or silk and wool, then later made of cotton and wool, or of just wool.

September 11, 1817. A slave named Isaac escaped from the Wilson County plantation of William Sweatt. Sweatt said in his statement that Isaac was "about three-quarters white," and that he had red hair and freckles.

Isaac stood about 5'6", and he had been marked with a "notch in his right ear."

When he ran, Isaac was wearing a cotton shirt, striped cotton overalls and a wool hat.

Sweatt expected Isacc to try to pass himself off as a free man named John Pate. Sweat offered $20 for Isaac's return.

On September 17, Isaac was captured and lodged in the Robertson County jail by jailer William Crunk. Just as predicted, Issac had tried to pass himself off as John Pate. However, when captured, he admitted to being William Sweatt's slave.

Crunk requested that Sweatt come to Robertson County, pay the jail fee, and take Isaac away.

Source: *The Nashville Whig and the Tennessee Advertiser*, September 29, 1817.

September 15, 1817. Several petitions were delivered to the state legislature requesting that it promote the emancipation of Tennessee's slaves.

Source: Office of Tennessee Secretary of State, *Tennessee Legislative Petitions*.

September 15, 1817. The Manumission Society presented a memorial to the Tennessee legislature asking it to seriously consider the many petitions calling for:

1. the abolition of slavery.
2. Petitions requesting laws prohibiting slave traffic across the state.
3. Petitions requesting legislation granting slaveholders the permission to free their slaves if those slaves were capable of making a living for themselves.

Source: Office of Tennessee Secretary of State, *Tennessee Legislative Petitions*.

Note: The Manumission Society was a collection of groups, usually founded by Quakers or other religious organizations, whose goal was the abolition of slavery by legal, nonviolent means.

September 23, 1817. Stump, Tilford & Company were hiring 20 or 30 slaves to work for one year at Cumberland Saline in Jackson County, Tennessee. Cumberland Saline was already in operation, and it had the capacity to supply Jackson County and adjacent counties with salt.

Source: *The Nashville Whig and Tennessee Advertiser*, September 29, 1817.

September 29, 1817. James Jackson and Sarah Hanna, the executors of the James Hanna estate, sold his property. Included in the sale were "a first rate" man slave, two women slaves, and six slave children.

The executors accepted credit for purchases over $10 and they gave buyers nine months to pay.

Source: *The Nashville Whig and Tennessee Advertiser*, September 22, 1817.

October 27, 1817. In the Tennessee State House Representative Trimble presented an amendment to the bill entitled "A bill more efficiently to provide for the trial of slaves." The amendment read:

That in all cases where a jury shall find a slave guilty of an offense, the punishment of which is death, said jury shall assess the value of such slave, and if such slave shall be executed, in pursuance of a sentence pronounced upon such finding, it shall be lawful for the owner of such slave, to receive out of the treasury of this state, a sum equal to two thirds of the value of such slave.

The vote on the amendment was 20 yes, and 20 no. Thus, it failed. The bill without the amendment failed as well. Eventually, he legislature did approve paying slave holders for legally executed slaves.

Source: *The Nashville Whig and Tennessee Advertiser*, November 17, 1817.

November 4, 1817. The Tennessee legislature created House Committee on the Abolition of Slavery. Committee Chairman, Representative Willis reported the position of the committee.

The Committee held that no steps had been taken "preparatory to the immediate, or gradual emancipation of slaves and that any attempt to accomplish that objective, without the use of preparatory means would be premature." He continued that "a premature attempt would probably be productive of pernicious consequences," for the slaves and the general population as well.

The committee also held that separating married slaves and slaves from their children should be continued to be allowed. To forbid separating slave families was, in the committee's view, bad business.

Additionally, the committee didn't believe a law requiring slaveholders to "furnish their slaves with suitable provisions, clothing," and housing was necessary. Thus, slaveholders could treat their slaves any way they wished.

The committee did want some changes to the slave laws. It endorsed the idea of the creation of an African colony to accept emancipated American slaves. Likewise, the committee agreed with the idea of prohibiting the importation of slaves from other states into Tennessee.

On November 7, the bill to prohibit the importation of slaves into Tennessee failed to pass.

Sources: *The Nashville Whig and Tennessee Advertiser*, November 4, 1817; Source: *The Nashville Whig and Tennessee Advertiser*, November 17, 1817.

December 15, 1817. A slave named Jim escaped from Samuel Hodge's plantation near Pond Lick in Wilson County. Jim was about 24, and he stood about 5'6". An African by birth, Jim spoke poorly and his teeth had been filed down in the custom of the tribe from which he came. Jim also had "peculiar" tribal marks on his chest.

Hodge believed that Jim was still "lurking" around the Wilson County area, and he offered a $50 reward for the runaway's return.

Source: *The Nashville Whig and the Tennessee Advertiser*, September 26, 1817.

December 17, 1817. The executors of the estate of the late Dr. Francis May of Nashville sold his property. Among other items, several slaved were auctioned.

Source: *The Nashville Whig and Tennessee Advertiser*, December 8, 1817.

December 23, 1817. Edward Ward, W. C. Ward, and B. B. Jones were the executors of the William Dickson estate. In that role, they met a group of Nashvillians and hired out a group of slaves consisting of men, women, boys, and girls for all of 1818.

The executors "earnestly requested" that those they hired the slaves to return them well-clothed and on time.

Source: *The Nashville Whig and Tennessee Advertiser*, December 15, 1817.

1818

January 2, 1818. A slave named Pompey escaped from the Benjamin Phillips plantation eight miles south of Nashville. Pompey was 26 or 27 and he stood about 5'10". Pompey had a history of escaping.

Phillips offered a $10 reward if Pompey was returned to the plantation, or $20 if the runaway was lodged elsewhere.

Source: *The Nashville Whig and the Tennessee Advertiser*, January 5, 1818.

January 26, 1818. By order of the Davidson County Court, the John Erwin estate was sold at the Nashville Courthouse. Five slaves were auctioned including two men, one woman, and two male youths.

Source: *The Nashville Whig and Tennessee Advertiser*, January 24, 1818.

January 29, 1818. The guardians of the heirs of the late Burris Harris estate sold his slaves at his property on the Harpeth River in Dickson County. Most of the men and women sold were young, and several children were sold as well. Buyers were given a year to pay.

Source: *The Nashville Whig and Tennessee Advertiser*, January 24, 1818.

February 14, 1818. The Robertson & Curry Company sold several stills, kegs, and other items. Additionally, they sold an older man slave, as well as a slave boy who was 10 or 11 years of age. Buyers had 90 days to pay.

Source: *The Nashville Whig and Tennessee Advertiser*, February 7, 1818.

February 24, 1818. A slave named Ned escaped from the John Harding estate on Richland Creek, nine miles from Nashville. Ned was 21 or 22, he stood about 5'9" inches tall, and he was stout.

When he escaped, Ned was wearing a white hat, an old, dark colored overcoat with a large cape, black colored velvet pantaloons, a homespun cotton coat, and a calico-colored waistcoat. He also had other clothes with him. He left astride a handsome, eight-year-old bay horse.

Harding had bought Ned from a slave dealer named John S. Butler only four days before. Butler had purchased Ned from a man named Hamblin on February 1, near Rogersville in Hawkins County, Tennessee. Harding believed that Ned was trying to get back to the Hamblin plantation.

Harding offered a $40 reward for the return of Ned and the horse, or $20 for either.

Source: *The Nashville Whig and the Tennessee Advertiser*, March 7, 1818.

March 11, 1818. C. D. McLean of Nashville wanted to hire a slave boy for the remainder of 1818.

Source: *The Nashville Whig and Tennessee Advertiser*, March 21, 1818.

March 12, 1818. A slave named Anthony either escaped or was stolen from the plantation belonging to Henry Basinger. Anthony was about 40, light complexioned and he had a large scar on one of his cheeks. Additionally, Anthony was identifiable by the fact that he was missing part of his index finger on his right hand.

When he left, Anthony was wearing a blue homespun coat.

Anthony's wife was enslaved on a nearby plantation and Basinger had let him go alone to visit her. Anthony had never returned, and Basinger thought the slave may have been stolen.

Basinger purchased Anthony from Joseph Wilson, but there was some question as to if Anthony had been stolen some years before, and then the thief had sold him.

Regardless of legal ownership, Basinger offered "a generous reward" of $20 for Anthony's return, and $100 if the slave stealer was captured.

Source: *The Nashville Whig and the Tennessee Advertiser*, March 28, 1818.

March 21, 1818. N. Tilford of Murfreesboro had a piece of property and a dwelling for sale. Tilford said he'd accept land, slaves, merchandise, or bank stock in payment.

Source: *The Nashville Whig and Tennessee Advertiser*, March 28, 1818.

April 18, 1818. Governments also employed slave labor from time to time. The city of Nashville paid John Mayfield $41 for the hire of a slave.

Source: *The Nashville Whig and Tennessee Advertiser*, May 15, 1819.

May 1, 1818. A slave woman named Sucky escaped with her two-year-old child from the D. L. Thompson plantation in Nashville. Thompson had hired Sucky from the estate of the late R. Cross.

Sucky was wearing a man's blue checkered coat when she ran away.

Several of Sucky's adult children had also been hired out, and Thompson believed that one of them was harboring her. He "respectfully requested" that those who had hired Sucky's children not let her come into their kitchens at night and get food. Thompson also offered an undetermined reward to anyone who caught and held Sucky until he could get her.

Source: *The Nashville Whig and the Tennessee Advertiser*, May 9, 1818.

May 2, 1818. The Robertson & Curry Company sold three slaves for a person who was moving to Philadelphia.

One slave was 25. He was an "excellent coachman, hostler, and complete house servant," and a "tolerable cook." He was "sober, honest, and well-disposed."

Another slave sold was a woman of about 45 years. She was "a good plain and pastry cook, a good laundry woman and ironer." She was also "of good character."

The third slave was a girl of about 10-years-old. She was used as a nursemaid, and she could spin. She was very obedient and smart.

Source: *The Nashville Whig and Tennessee Advertiser*, May 9, 1818.

Note: A hostler was a person who cared for horses and mules.

May 10, 1818. Three slaves escaped from the Allen Elston plantation on Cain Creek in Lincoln County, Tennessee.

One slave was named Moses, one was named Ben, and one was named Dick. Elston claimed ownership of Moses and Ben, but he had just rented Dick from Benjamin Short.

Moses was 23, He was slender, and he stood about 5'9". He had a "notable" scar above one of his eyes.

When he left, Moses was wearing a black, broadcloth coat, a pair of blue colored woolen pantaloons, a striped swansdown vest partially made of cotton, and a good roram hat.

Ben was about 18, and he was about the same height as Moses was. Ben was light complexioned and he was knocked kneed.

When Ben left, he was wearing an old woolen hat.

Dick was about the same height as the other two slaves, but he was heavier than they were.

When he ran away, Dick was wearing cotton clothing.

Elston believed a white man had stolen the three slaves. He offered $50 to anyone capturing the slaves.

Source: *The Nashville Whig and the Tennessee Advertiser*, May 30, 1818.

Note: Broadcloth was smooth-faced material used for men's garments, usually of double width.

Note: A swansdown vest was another name for waistcoat.

Note: A Roram hat is a head covering made from woolen cloth with a fur face.

May 15, 1818. At 10 a.m., the executors of the late John Walker's estate sold all his livestock, horses, cattle, sheep, and household furniture. Additionally, they sold eight slaves belonging to the estate. The sellers offered credit to those with security.

Source: *The Nashville Whig and Tennessee Advertiser*, April 25, 1818.

July 6, 1818. A slave woman named Luce escaped from the Francis Baley plantation in Warren County, Tennessee. Lucy was between the ages of 20 and 25, she was light complexioned, and she had a "fierce look." Luce was heavyset, and her head and both her arms were scarred, supposedly from being scalded.

Baley offered a $50 reward for Luce's return.

Source: *The Nashville Whig and the Tennessee Advertiser*, October 24, 1818.

September 24, 1818. Humphries County jailer, Joshua Williams, reported that he had jailed a runaway slave at Reynoldsburg, Tennessee. The detained man identified himself as Harry and he said he had escaped from the James O'Neal plantation in Maury County, about four miles from Columbia.

Williams requested that O'Neal come to the jail and get Harry.

Source: *The Nashville Whig and the Tennessee Advertiser*, October 10, 1818.

Note: Until 1837, Reynoldsburg was the county seat of Humphries County. The original site of Reynoldsburg is now submerged beneath Kentucky Lake.

October 15, 1818. Nashville attorney John H. Eaton was the trustee of the $1,500 loan made to Alexander W. Jones. When the debt wasn't repaid, Eaton supervised a sale of some of the slaves Jones held. The sale took place at the Davidson County Courthouse. The names of the slaves sold were John, Lucky, Kesiah, Joseph, Lucy, Hanna, Will, and David.

About a month after the auction, Eaton became a United States Senator.

Source: *The Nashville Whig and Tennessee Advertiser*, October 3, 1818.

Note: John Henry Eaton (1790-1856) was a prominent political figure associated closely with Andrew Jackson. He served in the US Senate, as US Secretary of War, Governor of Florida Territory, and US Minister to Spain.

October 18, 1818. George Shall and B. Poyzer reported the escape of a husband-and-wife pair of slaves.

The husband was named Francis. He was about 34, and he stood about 5'7". He had recently recovered from smallpox and his face was disfigured badly by it. Francis was smart and artistic. He was usually mild, but he enjoyed drinking and when he was drunk, he was talkative.

When he ran away, Francis took several articles of clothing with him, including a blue "close coat of super fine cloth," and a faded olive-green frockcoat.

Francis claimed to be an equine specialist, and when he ran away, he took with him a "very fine" dark bay horse with a bobbed tail. Francis also took a saddle, a bridle, and three pairs of saddle bags.

The wife was named Maria (sometimes called Kesiah). She was about 26, and she stood about 5'4". She had thick, long hair and a large mouth.

When she left, she had a black beaver hat with black feathers, a black silk bonnet, as well as other superior quality clothing.

Maria had excellent manners, was talkative, and she smiled a great deal.

Maria had children enslaved in the Duck River area and the slavers thought she and Francis might try to go there, or that they might attempt to go to Ohio, Indiana, or Illinois.

The slavers offered $250 for the return of the couple, or $200 for Francis alone, or $50 for Maria alone, if caught outside Tennessee. They offered half the reward if their capture took place in Tennessee. An additional $50 was offered for the horse.

Source: *The Nashville Whig and the Tennessee Advertiser*, October 24, 1818.

Note: A frockcoat was a formal coat for men. It came down to about the knee.

November 14, 1818. Theodore Shackleford wanted to rent two of his plantations about three miles from Nashville. Each of his plantations had about 100 acres of cleared land. Additionally, he wanted to hire an overseer for his other plantation. He also wanted to rent several slaves to work as field hands.

Source: *The Nashville Whig and Tennessee Advertiser*, November 14, 1818.

November 14, 1818. The Dunn & Phillips Auction Company of Mansker's Lick in Davidson County sold a slave and her child. Both slaves were in excellent condition.

The woman was about 31. She was very trustworthy, a good house servant, understood cooking, and she was a good at doing laundry and weaving.

The boy was about four-years-old.

Source: *The Nashville Whig and Tennessee Advertiser*, November 14, 1818.

November 21, 1818. Sarah McLean, who lived three miles east of Nashville, had three slaves to hire out. She had husband and wife slaves that she would only hire out together, and another man that she would hire out separately. McLean related that she would give preference to when hiring the slaves "to those residing in the country."

Source: *The Nashville Whig and Tennessee Advertiser*, November 21, 1818.

December 9, 1818. The executors of the Robert Cartwright estate sold his large 720-acre plantation. It was located about 10 miles from Nashville and about two miles from the Cumberland River. They also sold 10 slaves, one of whom was "an excellent distiller."

Source: *The Nashville Whig and Tennessee Advertiser*, November 21, 1818.

December 10, 1818. Ilai Metcalf lived at Neely's Bend near the mouth of Stones River. Metcalf sold a wide variety of items.

Additionally, Metcalf hired out a number of slaves for all of 1819. Among the slaves he hired out were men who were good stone masons, brick makers, brick layers. He also had boys, and women to hire out.

Source: *The Nashville Whig and Tennessee Advertiser*, October 24, 1818.

1819

January 1, 1819. C. Y, Hooper wanted to rent his plantation three miles north of Nashville. His slaves were part of the rental agreement.

Source: *The Nashville Whig and Tennessee Advertiser*, November 21, 1818.

January 1, 1819. During an event at the Nashville Courthouse, the executors of the late W. Hobson estate rented eight or ten adult slaves. One was a blacksmith, one a carpenter, and several were "first-rate" sawyers.

Source: *The Nashville Whig and Tennessee Advertiser*, December 19, 1818.

January 1, 1819. Roger B. Sapping was seeking an overseer for his plantation. Sapping offered to pay good wages, but he wanted an overseer who was "industrious and sober." Sapping required applicants to provide references.

Source: *The Nashville Whig and Tennessee Advertiser*, February 27, 1819.

January 20, 1819. A slave named Gere escaped from the William McCann plantation on Browns Creek about three miles south of Nashville. Gere was "smart and sensible." He was about 28, and he stood about 5'10". His eyes were large and his face was long. His nose was "not very flat." Gere's toes turned in when he walked and one of his fingers was crooked at the first joint.

When he ran away, Gere was wearing a green bombazine coatee, but since then he had been seen wearing a coatee and overalls died with walnut bark.

McCann believed that Gere would try to steal a horse and get to one of the Free States. He offered a reward of $40 to anyone who returned Gere if the runaway was captured out of state. If Gere were found and detained in Tennessee, McCann promised that he would pay a reward of $20.

Source: *The Nashville Whig and the Tennessee Advertiser*, January 30, 1819.

January 21, 1819. Representatives of General Chamberlain Jones of Virginia brought several slaves to Chandler's Cotton Factory near Clover Bottom in Davidson County and hired them out. The dates of hire ran until October 25, 1819.

Those hired out included men, women, and boys. Among the men was a blacksmith, several waggoners, and a number of plowmen. Some of the women were good cooks and house servants. All the slaves hired out were experienced at working in the tobacco fields.

Source: *The Nashville Whig and Tennessee Advertiser*, January 16, 1819.

January 27, 1819. J. P. McConnell, the Lincoln County jailer at Fayetteville, locked up a slave named Harry. Harry said he belonged to Joseph Cook of Davidson County.

McConnell requested that Cook come to Fayetteville and get Harry.

Source: *The Nashville Whig and the Tennessee Advertiser*, February 6, 1819.

February 1, 1819. A slave named Willis escaped from Addison Benford's plantation in Davidson County. Willis was about 23 or 24, and he stood about 6'3". He was missing the end of one of his toes on his right foot.

Benford was offering a $50 reward for the return of Willis.

Source: *The Nashville Whig and the Tennessee Advertiser*, May 22, 1819.

February 4, 1819. John Hill of Rhea County captured two escaped slaves and jailer Jacob Brown incarcerated them at the county seat of Washington.

Brown said the two slaves had been stealing "pretty largely" in the area. They were caught with three dresses, two sherrivallies, one black velvet and one corduroy, a brass barreled pistol, a pair of lady's boots, and two cotton umbrellas.

One of the slaves was named Joe. He was between 25 and 30, and he was well put together. He had a scar over each eye, and another one under his left eye.

When he was captured, Joe was wearing a pair of cloth pantaloons, a striped swansdown vest, a pale blue cloth coat and a green surtout coat. Joe said he grew up on the Ellis Putney plantation in Buckingham County, Virginia and was sent west with Robert Bundrum.

The other slave was named Sam. He was short and stout. His face was covered with "bumps."

When he was arrested, Sam was wearing a blue coat and pantaloons. Sam said he belonged to a man from Virginia, but not to Robert Bundrum.

Brown encouraged the owners of the runaways to come forward, pay the charges, and take them away from the jail.

Source: *The Nashville Whig and the Tennessee Advertiser*, March 20, 1819.

Note: Sherrivallies were men's pants that resembled military trousers.

Note: A surtout coat was an overcoat similar to a frockcoat.

Note: Washington (now called "Old Washington") was the Rhea County seat of government until 1889.

February 9, 1819. At Springfield, Tennessee a slave woman and her child were sold as part of the estate of the late William

Henrey. The woman was between 20 and 35, and the child was about five-years-old.

Source: *The Nashville Whig and Tennessee Advertiser*, January 2, 1819.

February 10, 1819. A slave named John escaped from F. Thorton's plantation five miles from Springfield, in Robertson County, Tennessee. John was 24, stood about 5'10", had a light complexion, a thin face, and he suffered from tooth decay.

Thorton said that anyone returning John would be "liberally reward."

Source: *The Nashville Whig and the Tennessee Advertiser*, February 27, 1819.

February 13, 1819. Five slaves (men and women) who were part of the Nathan Peeples estate were auctioned off at the Courthouse in Nashville. The sellers gave buyers nine months to pay.

Source: *The Nashville Whig and Tennessee Advertiser*, January 30, 1819.

February 14, 1819. Mark Ramey locked up a slave named Carter in the Davidson County jail. Carter was about 5'8", and strongly he was built. He had small scars over his left eye, on his right nostril, and on his upper lip.

Carter said he belonged to Martial Smith of Fauquier, Virginia. Carter related that he was one of more than 20 slaves Smith was taking to Natchez, Mississippi, but that he had managed to escape captivity near Huntsville, Alabama Territory.

Ramey requested that Smith come to Nashville, pay the jail fees, and get Carter.

Source: *The Nashville Whig and the Tennessee Advertiser*, February 27, 1819.

February 20, 1819. Administrators of the late Colonel Bedford Brown's estate brought 25 slaves to the Saunders & Chandler store in Davidson County and sold them. The slaves included men, women, boys, and girls.

Source: *The Nashville Whig and Tennessee Advertiser*, February 6, 1819.

February 27, 1819. A slave dealer named John S. Butler of Davidson County had three slaves for sale. Two were boys, each of whom were 12 or 13, and one was a girl of about 18. Butler was willing to give short-term credit to buyers.

On April 3, Butler put two other young slaves up for sale. As always, he said he would accept cash for them, or he would give short-term credit.

Sources: *The Nashville Whig and Tennessee Advertiser*, February 27, 1819; *The Nashville Whig and Tennessee Advertiser*, April 3, 1819.

March 1, 1819. The estate of the late Major Plummer Willis was sold at his home in Robertson County. Along with stills, cattle, hogs, and furniture, 10 or 12 slaves were auctioned.

Source: *The Nashville Whig and Tennessee Advertiser*, February 27, 1819.

March 13, 1819. Eight slaves were auctioned off at the Davidson County Courthouse in Nashville. Those sold included three men between the ages of 17 and 20, three girls between the ages of 12 and 15, and a 28-year-old woman with her four-year-old child.

Source: *The Nashville Whig and Tennessee Advertiser*, March 6, 1819.

March 19, 1819. Peyton Robertson had several slaves for sale at his plantation four miles south of Nashville. Robertson offered buyers 60 or 90 days of credit.

Source: *The Nashville Whig and Tennessee Advertiser*, March 20, 1819.

March 27, 1819. Nashvillian John Brown needed money. In order to get funds, he was selling a slave woman. She was about 40, trustworthy and a good housekeeper. Brown wanted to sell her to a local person and not to a speculator that would resell her for profit.

Source: *The Nashville Whig and Tennessee Advertiser*, March 27, 1819.

March 27, 1819. Z. W. Waters of Richland Creek, five miles west of Nashville, was selling five young slaves. Two of the slaves were men, one 18 and the other 20. The other three were girls, one 10, one 15, and one 18.

Source: *The Nashville Whig and Tennessee Advertiser*, March 27, 1819.

April 12, 1819. Riley Slocumb reported that a slave named Peter had escaped from his plantation near the city of Franklin, in Williamson County, Tennessee. Peter was 36 or 37, he stood about 5'10", was thin, and had a light complexion. He was a good shoemaker.

When he ran away, Peter was wearing a homemade dark green hunting shirt, a pair of green cotton overalls, and a striped cotton waistcoat. He also had a pair of velvet overalls with him.

Slocumb accused Peter of stealing two silver watches with steel chains. One of the watches had the initials "S.P." engraved on it. Slocumb promised that anyone who caught Peter would be "well-rewarded for his trouble."

Source: *The Nashville Whig and the Tennessee Advertiser*, May 1, 1819.

April 15, 1819. A slave named Lewis escaped from Robert Johnston's Davidson County plantation. Johnston didn't claim ownership of Lewis. He had hired Lewis from a slaveholder.

Lewis was about 30, stood 5'10", had a round face, a large nose, and small dark eyes. Lewis was pleasant acting and was quick to smile. On the other hand, he was a heavy drinker.

When he ran away, Lewis was wearing a white hat, a brown frockcoat, a striped waistcoat, and a close body coat.

Johnston believed that Lewis left on horseback with an Irishman named Black. Black and Lewis were traveling as master and slave.

Black was evidently from New Orleans. He was between 25 and 30 years old, of average size, had black hair, had a thin, pockmarked face and a sharp nose.

Black was wearing a dark blue coat and pantaloons. Black had supposedly told others that he was on his way to Pennsylvania. If that was true, his intent was to either sell Lewis along the way, or to free him.

Johnston promised that if Lewis were captured by October, he would pay a reward of one of the following values: $75 to anyone delivering Lewis to Nashville; $40 of the runaway was jailed within 200 miles of Nashville; or $20 if Lewis were captured more than 200 miles away. He did not offer a reward for Black's capture.

Source: *The Nashville Whig and the Tennessee Advertiser*, May 1, 1819.

April 22, 1819. A slave named Harry escaped from Washington Pulliam's plantation six miles south of Nashville. Henry was about 5'6", and he was very bowlegged.

When he left, Harry was wearing a black roundabout, brown homespun pantaloons, and a wool hat. Harry had only recently been brought to Tennessee from Virginia, and Pulliam felt he the runaway might try to go back there.

Pulliam offered $10 for Harry's return.

Source: *The Nashville Whig and the Tennessee Advertiser*, May 1, 1819.

May 1, 1819. A slave named Nelly escaped from Major Joel Dyer's plantation in Murfreesboro. Nelly was about 17, but she looked younger. Nelly grew up in Kingston, Tennessee, and was brought to Murfreesboro in the summer of 1818.

Nelly had relations in Nashville and Dyer surmised that she may have gone to them. He offered a $25 reward for her return.

Source: *The Nashville Whig and the Tennessee Advertiser*, September 4, 1819.

May 8, 1819. A slave named Harry escaped from the custody of Davidson County Sheriff, Thomas Hickman, at the Courthouse in Nashville. Harry was about 28 or 30, stood about 5'10", was squarely made, and light complexioned. Alexander McDowell claimed ownership of Harry.

Sheriff Hickman offered a $10 reward for Harry.

Source: *The Nashville Whig and the Tennessee Advertiser*, May 8, 1819.

May 29, 1819. A Nashvillian wanted to purchase two slaves – a man and a woman.

Source: *The Nashville Whig and Tennessee Advertiser*, June 5, 1819.

June 4, 1819. Edmund, a slave on the John Camp plantation at Elkton, Giles County, Tennessee escaped. Edmund was 22-years-old and below average in size.

Edmund was a proud man, and he was fond of nice clothes. He was a good fiddle player, and he was a carpenter by trade.

Camp offered $100 as a reward if Edmund were taken into custody more than 150 miles from Elkton, and $50 if the runaway was captured closer than that.

Source: *The Nashville Whig*, October 20, 1819.

July 5, 1819. The Davidson County Sheriff put seven slaves up for auction at Stump's Tavern on Whites Creek. John Stump claimed ownership of them, but the Davidson County Circuit Court ordered that the sale of the slaves to pay the debt Stump's debts to Richard Hyde. The Tennessee Court of Appeals upheld the ruling.

Those sold were a man named Matt who was about 40; Matt's wife Dafney, who was about 30; Daniel, age 15; Ferriby, age 12; Sam, who was six; Huldy, an infant; and Milley, who was 23.

Source: *The Nashville Whig and Tennessee Advertiser*, July 10, 1819.

August 20, 1819. A slave named Paris escaped from the W. B. Lewis plantation about a mile and one-half from Nashville. Paris was 27 or 28, he stood about 5'8", was stout, and he spoke slowly.

Lewis believed that Paris was in the company of others and that they would try to get him to Ohio. Lewis based his belief on the fact that Paris had escaped in December 1818 and had headed north before being captured in Glasgow, Kentucky.

Lewis offered a $50 reward for anyone that returned Paris to him.

Source: *The Nashville Whig*, November 25, 1819.

August 28, 1819. A Nashvillian had a slave of about 30 years of age for sale, and two others for hire.

Source: *The Nashville Whig and Tennessee Advertiser*, August 28, 1819.

August 31, 1819. Dickson County jailer, C. Robertson, arrested and locked up a slave named John. John was about 25, small, well-built, and chunky. He bore scars from several floggings he had received from his slaveholder.

John said he belonged to John Gordon of Sumner County. Robertson requested that Gordon come to Dickson County, prove title to John, pay the jail fee, and take the runaway slave with him.

Source: *The Nashville Whig*, September 4, 1819.

September 2, 1819. A slave named Abner escaped from John Templeton's plantation in Bedford County, about seven miles south of Columbia, Tennessee. Abner was about 21, stood about 5'8", and he weighed about 140 pounds. He was light complexioned, and he was highly intelligent.

When he left, Abner was wearing a red coat made from yarn, and a cloth waistcoat. However, he had certainly changed clothes after he ran away.

Abner got away aboard a bay horse and Templeton offered $100 to get the runaway and the horse back.

Source: *The Nashville Whig*, September 25, 1819.

September 6, 1819. A slave named George escaped from the Michael Campbell plantation. George was 26 or 27, and he stood about 5'9". George had a large scar on his face caused by a gunpowder burn several years earlier, and he had the bumps caused by the burn cut off to make him appear less disfigured. He was very athletic and was known for his running ability.

George's wife was enslaved on the Sim plantation about five miles from Nashville, and Campbell expected the runaway to go there. Campbell offered a $50 reward if Adam was returned from out of state and $10 if he was captured in Tennessee.

Source: *The Nashville Whig*, September 18, 1819.

September 8, 1819. White County, Tennessee jailor, John B. Garrett, placed a slave named Luke behind bars in Sparta. Luke was between 25 and 30, and he stood about six feet tall. The runaway was "remarkably knock-kneed" and he moved about awkwardly.

When he was captured, Luke was wearing a pair of corded pantaloons and a great coat that was dark in color.

Luke said he belonged to James Hood. Hood lived about two miles from Florence, Alabama Territory and had been searching for Luke since at least June 2.

Garrett requested that Hood come to Sparta and get Luke.

Source: *The Nashville Whig*, October 2, 1819.

September 11, 1819. A slave named Adam escaped from the plantation owned by Peter Moseley in Wilson County. Adam was about 35 and he stood about 5'10". A piece of one of Adam's ears had been bitten off. Adam was also missing some of his front teeth.

Moseley had purchased Adam from the Stump & Daniel Company and before that Adam had belonged to a Mr. Paine of Jonesboro, Tennessee. Moseley believed that Adam was trying to get back there.

Moseley offered a "generous reward" for Adam's capture or return.

Source: *The Nashville Whig*, September 11, 1819.

September 11, 1819. James Potts had two slaves for sale. One was a woman. She was good at cooking, doing laundry, and ironing. The other was a young man of 18 or 19 years.

Source: *The Nashville Whig*, September 11, 1819.

September 14, 1819. A slave named Simon escaped from D. Vaughn's plantation. Simon was an old man and he was "lame in one of his hips." When he ran away, Simon was wearing a white, woolen homemade coat.

Vaughn was offering a $10 reward for Simon's return.

Source: *The Nashville Whig*, October 20, 1819.

Note: Most runaway slaves were young. It was unusual for an older slave to try to escape, but it did happen occasionally.

September 20, 1819. There were many petitions, each bearing several signatures asking the legislature to enact laws allowing slaveholders who desired to do to free their slaves.

Source: Office of Tennessee Secretary of State, *Tennessee Legislative Petitions*.

September 20, 1819. A petition from Blount County accompanied by 202 signatures requested that the legislature abolish slavery.

Source: Office of Tennessee Secretary of State, *Tennessee Legislative Petitions*.

September 20, 1819. Another petition was presented to the legislature asking it to develop a plan to abolish slavery.

Source: Office of Tennessee Secretary of State, *Tennessee Legislative Petitions*.

September 21, 1819. William Green was enroute from Warren, North Carolina to Lawerence County, Alabama Territory with a slave named Guilford. Somewhere near the Rock Island between the Tennessee towns of Sparta and McMinnville, Guilford made an escape. Guilford was 17 or 18, and he had a light complexion.

When he ran away, Guilford was wearing a black hat, a round jacket, a swansdown waistcoat, and homespun pantaloons with patches on both knees.

Green believed that Guilford might try to get back to North Carolina. He offered a $25 reward to get Guilford back.

Source: *The Nashville Whig*, December 8, 1819.

September 29, 1819. White County, Tennessee jailor, John B. Garrett, locked up another slave. The arrested slave was named Tom. He was about 40, he stood about 5'9", and his face was covered with smallpox scars. Additionally, he had an upper front tooth missing.

When he was arrested, Tom was wearing a green broadcloth coat, but he also had other clothes with him.

Tom said he was a carpenter and that he belonged to a man in Lebanon named John Banks.

Garrett requested that Banks come to Sparta and get Tom.

Source: *The Nashville Whig*, October 2, 1819.

October 26, 1819. Robertson County Sheriff Henry Frey jailed a slave woman named Dolly. Dolly was about 30 and she was average size.

Dolly was intelligent and well educated. According to Frey, she appeared to "understand business of almost any kind."

Dolly said she belonged to a Frenchman in New Orleans named Sopan, and Frey requested that Sopan come to the jail, prove his claim to Dolly, and take custody of her.

Source: *The Nashville Whig*, April 12, 1820.

November 13, 1819. The Tennessee House of Representatives established a select committee that received a memorial from several citizens calling for the abolition of slavery in the state.

Committee members were not ready to recommend abolition, but Representative Miller of the committee offered a resolution as a first step toward it. Miller's resolution would have allowed slaveholders "who are disposed to emancipate their slaves be permitted to do so without security on the part of the owners thereof."

Tennessee lawmakers were in no mood to make it easier for slaveholders to emancipate slaves and they voted down the resolution overwhelmingly by a vote of 26 to 3.

Source: *The Nashville Whig*, November 13, 1819.

November 24, 1819. A Nashvillian had a "smart and valuable" slave for sale. The reason for the sale was that the slaveholder couldn't afford to keep the slave any longer.

The slaveholder said the man wouldn't be sold to those "who buy to carry down the river." In other words, the slaveholder didn't want the man to fall into the clutches of a speculator.

Source: *The Nashville Whig*, November 24, 1819.

December 15, 1819. A slave named Dave escaped from the William B. Robertson plantation six miles west of Nashville. Dave stood about 5'10", he was bald, he had a pockmarked face, and his eyes weren't "very clear."

Robertson has purchased Dave from John Stump, but he expected the runaway slave to try to get to a Free State. With that in mind, Robertson offered a $200 reward for Dave if he were captured on the "west side" of the Ohio River; $100 if he were captured on the "east side" of the river, outside the state of Tennessee; or $50 if he were detained within state borders.

Source: *The Nashville Whig*, September 5, 1820.

December 27, 1819. A slave named Jack escaped from John Holcombe's plantation in Lincoln County. Jack was 31 or 32. He was large, had broad shoulders, had a light complexion, and he suffered from a speech impediment. He was a skilled whipsaw user and was a good shoemaker. However, was also a heavy drinker.

When Jack left, he was wearing a green homespun coat, a pair of black woolen pantaloons, an old woolen hat, and a pair of old shoes with new soles. He also took with him a new coat, a pair of velvet pantaloons, and a blanket.

Holcombe believed thar Jack might try to convince others that he was a free man, or that he might have obtained a pass. Jack was once the slave of Robert Boyd and Holcombe believed that Jack would try to go back to Boyd at Florence or Huntsville, Alabama. On the other hand, Holcombe thought that Jack might try to go in the opposite direction and try to get to Ohio.

Holcombe offered a $50 reward to get Jack back.

Source: *The Nashville Whig*, January 19, 1820.

December 31, 1819. The executors of Colonel Bedford Branen's estate brought a large number of slaves (men, women, boys, and girls) to Saunders & Chandler store and hired them out to the highest bidders.

Source: *The Nashville Whig*, November 24, 1819.

1820

January 5, 1820. J. B. West had a parcel of land, a dwelling with a detached kitchen, and several other buildings for sale on Summer Street in Nashville. West was willing to take cash, or cash and slaves, for the property.

Source: *The Nashville Whig*, January 5, 1820.

January 29, 1820. A slave named Peter escaped from Robert Smith's plantation on Fall Creek on Rutherford County. Peter was about 28. He stood about 5'10", was well-built, and he was round shouldered. Peter was smart and artistic. He could read well and write some.

When he ran away, Peter took a blue close-bodied coat of mixed cloth, a pair of double woven pantaloons, and two silk handkerchiefs. One handkerchief was black, and the other one was white with red polka dots.

Peter was believed to be using the papers of a free Black man by the name of Zachariah Bartlett, and Smith expected Peter to try to get to Ohio, Indiana, or Illinois.

Smith offered $15 for Peter's return.

Source: *The Nashville Whig*, May 10, 1820.

Note: Tennessee was one of three Slave States that never passed a law forbidding the teaching of slaves to read and write.

February 7, 1820. Sophia Perkins was the administratrix of the estate of the late W. Perkins. She auctioned off fatted steers, hogs, cows, furniture, and a slave called "Old Harry."

Source: *The Nashville Whig*, February 2, 1820.

February 9, 1820. Henry Rutherford was selling 200 acres of land, 100 acres of which were in cultivation. The plantation was on the main road 10 miles from Nashville, and it was eight miles from Franklin. Rutherford was selling the plantation for $25 per acre, and he was willing to accept payment in cash, in slaves, or in a combination of cash and slaves.

Source: *The Nashville Whig*, March 8, 1820.

February 10, 1820. Most of the property of the late Benjamin Philips was sold. Additionally, 30 slaves held by the estate were hired out to plantation owners.

Source: *The Nashville Whig*, February 2, 1820.

February 15, 1820. Some of the property of the late James P. Downs went on the auction block at the Nashville Courthouse. Three enslaved men, a bay mare, and two watches (one gold, and one silver), were sold. The seller offered credit to buyers.

Source: *The Nashville Whig*, February 2, 1820.

February 20, 1820. Sumner County Sheriff, A. H. Douglass, jailed a slave named Dick. Dick was about 21 and he said he belonged to Charles Briscoe of Maury County, Tennessee. Dick also said that Briscoe had purchased him from Samuel Keen of Lexington, Kentucky.

Douglass requested for the person with the legal claim to the slave, to come to Gallatin and get him.

Source: *The Nashville Whig*, June 21, 1820.

March 1, 1820. A. Richardson was looking to hire a slave between the ages of 18 and 20 to work on his farm.

Source: *The Nashville Whig*, March 1, 1820.

March 22, 1820. A Nashvillian wanted to purchase a slave that was "accustomed to housework."

Source: *The Nashville Whig*, March 22, 1820.

April 12, 1820. S. B. Marshall had a slave and a young horse for sale.

Source: *The Nashville Whig*, April 12, 1820.

April 12, 1820. A Nashvillian was selling a 19-year-old slave woman.

Source: *The Nashville Whig*, April 12, 1820.

May 3, 1820. A slave named Patrick escaped from J. H. Hall's plantation near Franklin, Tennessee atop a bay mare. Patrick stood about 5'10", and he had scar between his eyes. He was smart, artistic, and he was a good shoemaker.

Patrick left with one brown broadcloth suit, one dark suit made of mixed homespun material, and a brown overcoat.

Hall believed Patrick would either try to make his way to Ohio or try to get to his relations in Robertson County, Tennessee.

Hall offered a $50 reward if Patrick was delivered to him, or $25 if he had to go and retrieve the runaway.

Source: *The Nashville Whig*, May 17, 1820.

May 9, 1820. By virtue of a Tennessee Supreme Court ruling against him, all except four of the slaves held by Joel Lewis went to auction. R. McGavock, clerk of the Supreme Court, announced the sale.

Source: *The Nashville Whig*, April 19, 1820.

June 5, 1820. A slave named Phill escaped from R. Goodrich's plantation near Nashville. Phill was between 19 and 20, extremely tall and very skinny. Additionally, the well-spoken slave had a scar on his right jaw.

When he departed, Phill had a brown surcoat, blue broadcloth pantaloons, a linen shirt, a black cravat, and a fur hat.

Phill also took two race horses with him. One was a sorrel mare with a good saddle, and the other was a bay mare with a side saddle.

Goodrich offered $50 if Phill was returned to him, or $25 if he had to retrieve Phill from a jail.

Source: *The Nashville Whig*, June 5, 1820.

Note: A cravat is a short and wide strip of fabric worn by men around the neck and tucked inside an open-necked shirt.

June 9, 1820. A slave named Elijah escaped from the William Doake plantation in Lincoln County, about one mile from Fayetteville, Tennessee.

Elijah was 16-years-old, tall, and thin. When he left, his face was swollen by a tooth infection. He was a good brick molder.

Elijah ran away wearing a cotton shirt and pantaloons.

Doake said he believed that Elijah "fell in" with two waggoners near Fayetteville and went to Nashville with them. Then, according to Doake, Elijah likely took a keelboat captained by a man named Hanby, and he went on to New Orleans.

Doake offered $20 for Elijah's return.

Source: *The Nashville Whig*, June 28, 1820.

June 20, 1820. Isaac Hammer petitioned the state legislature requesting that it declare that all Black people in Tennessee were free.

Source: Office of Tennessee Secretary of State, *Tennessee Legislative Petitions*.

July 5, 1820. A Nashvillian want to hire out three slaves. Two were "first rate house servants." One of the house servants was an "excellent seamstress." The third slave was a 14-year-old girl.

Source: *The Nashville Whig*, July 5, 1820.

July 5, 1820. A Nashvillian offered to pay cash for two or three young slave women "of good character, and constitutions, and raised in the country."

Source: *The Nashville Whig*, July 5, 1820.

July 10, 1820. Four strong and healthy slaves escaped from the John Thompson plantation near Nashville.

Ben was about 22, and he stood about 5'9".

Davy was about 22, and he stood about 5'11".

Daniel was about 24, he stood about 5'10", and he was bow legged.

Aaron was about 25 and his height was about 5'7".

Thompson believed that the slaves would stay together and try to reach one of the Free States north of the Ohio River. He offered $25 each for their return.

Source: *The Nashville Whig*, July 12, 1820.

July 12, 1820. A slave named Sam escaped from J. B. Lanier's plantation in Charlotte, Tennessee. Sam was an intelligent man. He was about 22 or 23, he stood about 5'8", his face was pockmarked, and one of his arms had burn scars.

When he left, Sam had three pairs of pantaloons – one pair made of brown cloth and two pairs made of cotton. He took along a rifle and a silver watch, valued at $35 each.

Sam grew up on the Solomon Hall plantation about fifteen miles from Salisbury, North Carolina. Daniel Steele purchased Sam and brought him to Charlotte. Then Steele sold him to Lanier.

Sam had an inkstand with him and Lanier expected the slave to get or forge a pass, then try to use it to get back to North Carolina.

Lanier offered a $40 reward if Sam was captured outside Tennessee and $20 if he was detained within the state.

Source: *The Nashville Whig*, July 12, 1820.

July 15, 1820. A slave named Isaac escaped from the James Heflin plantation in Tuscaloosa County, Alabama. Isaac was 23 or 24 and small. He had a round scar on his forehead.

Issac had grown up on the John Rains Sr. plantation near Nashville, and Helfin had purchased Issac from John Rains Jr.

Heflin was certain that Isaac would do his best to get back to the Nashville area.

Heflin thought that Isaac either had a pass, was in the company of a white man, or was pretending to be a free man. He offered $20 to anyone who captured the runaway.

Source: *The Nashville Whig*, September 26, 1820.

July 29, 1820. The estate of the late Thomas B. Jones was sold in Giles County, Tennessee. Along with his personal possessions, and his livestock, a slave woman he had held was auctioned.

Source: *The Nashville Whig*, July 19, 1820.

August 9, 1820. A Nashvillian had a male slave for sale. The slave was about 20. He was smart, was an "excellent cook," and he had been used as a house servant for several years.

Source: *The Nashville Whig*, August 9, 1820.

August 23, 1820. The operators of the store that Thomas Hill had formerly managed had about $10,000 worth of dry goods and hardware for sale. The proprietors, A. Fisk and John C. Rhea, would give credit or would accept slaves in exchange for their merchandise.

Source: *The Nashville Whig*, August 23, 1820.

August 28, 1820. The Tennessee legislature passed an act stating that if real estate or slaves were sold by court order to settle debts, the person who owed the money could regain the real estate or slaves. According to the new law, if within two years of the forced sale, the person who owed the debt could prove the ability to repay the sales price at 10% per annum, the real estate or slaves would be returned to him.

Source: *The Nashville Whig*, August 9, 1820.

September 2, 1820. William B. Robertson had another slave escape. This slave, named Clem, was "a very remarkable fellow." Robertson had displayed a great deal of confidence in Clem. He had taken Clem with him on trips through several states – Free States and Slave States alike. They had even traveled along the Ohio River to Pittsburgh and back.

Robertson was certain that Clem would head north because the only reason he could have for running away was to gain his freedom.

Clem was at least six feet tall. His face was wide, his eyes were small and sunken into his head, and he had extremely large feet. Clem was noted for his strength and athleticism. He had wrestled several times and he had never lost to anyone "black or white." He was also a fast runner and a high jumper.

Clem left wearing an old fur hat, a brown broadcloth coat, a dark colored velvet roundabout, and a dark pair of twilled pantaloons made from either cotton or wool.

Robertson stated that Clem was on horseback. He wasn't sure what the horse looked like, but he was certain that the saddle Clem was using was old and torn across its seat, the stirrup leathers didn't match, one being broader than the other. The stirrup irons were old and they didn't match either. The saddle was covered with a buffalo robe that had been cut to fit it. The reins were red and had been "chewed."

Robertson was convinced that Clem would head north because the only reason he could have for running away was to gain his freedom. Robertson offered a $300 reward if Clem was captured on the west side of the Ohio River, and $100 if he were detained on the east side.

Source: *The Nashville Whig*, September 5, 1820.

September 2, 1820. Most of the late Foster Sawyer's property was sold at the Robertson & Curry Auction Store. However, some of the slaves were not sold. Sawyer's heirs hired several of them out for labor until December 25 of that year.

Source: *The Nashville Whig*, August 2, 1820.

September 2, 1820. There was an auction at the Nashville courthouse. Thomas Shackeford was moving from Nashville to

Missouri and he was disposing of his property. Three slaves were sold during the auction. One was a blacksmith; one was a carpenter; and one was adept at making and firing brick. Shackeford gave buyers six months to make full payment.

Source: *The Nashville Whig*, August 16, 1820.

September 4, 1820. Sheriff Henry Frye took a slave named Solomon into custody in Robertson County. Solomon was 23, about 5'10", and he had a scar over one eye.

Solomon said he belonged to Colonel Anthony Winston of Russell Valley, Alabama and Frey requested that Winston come to the jail and get the runaway.

Winston did take possession of Solomon. However, on October 1, Solomon escaped again.

When he ran away this time, Solomon was wearing a green cloth coat, and new homespun overalls.

Winston believed that Solomon would try to get to Middle Tennessee again and he offered $10 to get the runaway returned to him.

Sources: *The Nashville Whig*, October 3, 1820; *The Nashville Whig*, November 22, 1820.

September 19, 1820. Dickson County jailer, David Shropshire, said he had incarcerated a slave named John in the jail at Charlotte. John was 23 or 24, and he stood about five feet tall. He had a scar on the right side of his face near his ear. The scar was caused by a childhood burn.

John said he grew up on the Richard Harris plantation in Newberry County, South Carolina. John continued that Harris had sold him to Richard Poole and Samuel Farrar. John said that he ran away from the two slavers in Jackson County, Tennessee at Fort Blount during the spring of 1817, and that he had been on his own since.

Shropshire requested that those with a claim to John, come to Charolette with proof, and take him away.

Source: *The Nashville Whig*, September 19, 1820.

October 2, 1820. Thomas H. Meredith, Trustee of the Nathaniel Moody estate, sold a large amount of real estate, livestock, farming implements, and furniture at the Giles County courthouse in Pulaski.

Additionally, 12 slaves (men, women, boys, and girls) were sold during the auction. Meredith assured prospective buyers that the slaves were among the best in Tennessee.

Source: *The Nashville Whig*, September 26, 1820.

October 31, 1820. A Nashvillian wanted to purchase a slave girl of 17 or 18. However, he required that she be "well recommended" for her ability as a house servant. Moreover, he wanted a slave who could care for young children.

Source: *The Nashville Whig*, October 31, 1820.

November 25, 1820. Two slaves escaped from the jail in Columbia, Tennessee.

One slave was named George. He was about 40 and he stood about 5'8". George was fond of talking about his many travels.

George was wearing a blue pair of pantaloons, a swansdown vest, and a yellow jeans coat.

It was believed that George had papers that he intended to use to convince the authorities that he was a free man.

The other slave was named Jenny. She was about 35. She had a scar on her neck that appeared to have been made by a knife slash.

When she left the jail, Jenny had with her a white domestic frock, an interchangeable Levantine purple and red frockcoat, a plain white satin bonnet, a large blue and white shawl with a yellow striped border, a bundle of bed clothes, and a large carving knife with a white handle.

Joseph Royall wasn't interested in George, but he claimed title to Jenny. He offered a "liberal reward" for Jenny's return to his plantation on the Duck River in Bedford County.

The two runaways remained free for less than a month. On December 20, George and Jenny were captured in Hickman County, and county jailer, E. B. Hornbeak, locked them up.

George denied that he was a slave. He claimed to be a free man named George William Brown. He also claimed to be an itinerant preacher. Additionally, George told the jailer that his traveling companion was his wife. However, he couldn't prove anything he was saying.

For her part, Jenny didn't try to convince Hornbeak that she was a free person. She said she belonged to Joseph Royall. Hornbeak requested that those claiming title to the pair come to the jail, present their claims, and take possession if the runaways.

Sources: *The Nashville Whig*, November 29, 1820; *The Nashville Whig*, January 10, 1821.

November 27, 1820. A slave named Pompey, who sometimes called himself Pompey Williams, escaped from the F. E. Fisher plantation in Davidson County. Pompey was about 34, he stood about 5'10", and he was left-handed. Pompey was a shoemaker by trade, and he was an excellent workman.

When he ran away, Pompey was wearing a green bearskin cloth coat, and Russia duck pantaloons.

Pompey's wife was enslaved on a plantation in Franklin, and Fisher believed Pompey was hiding out there, or at Nashville. Fisher offered $100 for Pompey's return if he was captured out of state, or $50 if found in Tennessee.

Source: *The Nashville Whig*, November 27, 1820.

Note: Russia duck pantaloons were trousers made from a heavy linen fabric called "Russia duck." These pantaloons were strong and long-lasting. Often used by military forces because of their durability, they were also commonly issued to slaves.

December 4, 1820. A slave named Davy escaped from the Robertson County jail. Davy was about 30. He said he belonged to Blount Robertson, but before Robinson came for him, a white man helped him escape.

Sheriff Henry Frye offered $10 for Davy's return.

Source: *The Nashville Whig*, December 20, 1820.

December 30, 1820. On the Public Square in Nashville, all the slaves (men, women, and children) Dr. Young A. Gray held were sold. The purpose of the sale was to satisfy the doctor's creditors. Sold were men, women, and children.

Source: *The Nashville Whig*, December 20, 1820.

1821

January 1, 1821. Patrick H. Darby sold seven slaves at the courthouse in Springfield, Tennessee. One man sold was an "excellent distiller." Additionally, there were several slave girls ranging in age from 9 to 13.

Source: *The Nashville Whig*, December 6, 1820.

January 15, 1821. John C. Hall sold 181 acres, 65 acres which were cleared and fenced, a grist mill, a sawmill, and a distillery eight miles from Stewart's Ferry. Terms were one-third down and the balance in nine months to a year. Hall stated that he would accept cash, notes, or slaves as payment.

Source: *The Nashville Whig*, January 10, 1821.

March 24, 1821. Alpha Kingsley's property was sold at Nashville to settle his debts. Three slaves were sold as well. Their names were Jenny (a woman), Harriet (a girl), and Isam (a boy).

Source: *The Nashville Whig*, February 28, 1821.

April 4, 1821. West & Bradford of Nashville announced it would hold auctions on the first Monday of every month. Auctioning slaves was a big part of the company's business.

On July 25, West & Bradford sold six slaves on the Public Square in Nashville. There were three men between the ages of 21 and 38, two women between the ages of 20 and 30, and a child of 10 or 11.

Source: *The Nashville Whig*, April 4, 1821; *The Nashville Whig*, July 25, 1821.

April 22, 1821. Aaron Brown reported that two slaves had escaped from his plantation in Giles County, near Pulaski.

One of the slaves was named Abram. He was about 25, short of stature, and he had "large white eyes." Abram also had "knots or lumps" on his chest made by a whip during a beating he received from his slaveholder.

The other slave was named Hubbard. He was also about 25, and he was also short. Hubbard had a large scar on one side of his face caused by a burn.

The two runaways were in the company of three other people and Brown was certain that they were trying to get to one of the Free States. He offered a $100 reward if Abram and Hubbard were returned from out of state, and $50 if they were detained within Tennessee.

Source: *The Nashville Whig*, May 2, 1821.

April 30, 1821. A slave named Merit escaped from the John Davis plantation 11 miles south of Nashville. Merit was about 18, 5'8", he was awkward in speech and action, and he walked slowly. He rode away on bay mare.

Davis expected Merit to try to get to Indiana or Illinois. An unstated amount was offered for Merit's return.

Source: *The Nashville Whig*, May 9, 1821.

May 4, 1821. A slave named Fanny escaped from the Edward Scruggs plantation a mile above the mouth of Mansker's Creek in Sumner County. Fanny was between 35 and 40. She was a "very large sized woman," and she had a mole on her chin.

Fanny took a lot of clothing with her when she left.

Scruggs offered a $40 reward for Fanny if she was captured outside of Tennessee, and half that much if she was arrested in the state.

Source: *The Nashville Whig*, June 6, 1821.

May 7, 1821. A slave named Perry escaped from the plantation belonging to John Hightower in Williamson County about 11 miles from Nashville. Perry was about 40, and he stood about 5'7".

When Perry left, he took a suit of coarse green broadcloth, a pair of blue Nankeen, pantaloons, a pair of dressed buckskin pantaloons, two waistcoats, and a coarse woolen hunting shirt.

Hightower felt it was likely that Perry would try to get to one of the Free States, and he promised a reward for Perry's return.

Source: *The Nashville Whig*, May 30, 1821.

May 13, 1821. A slave named Levi escaped from the Austin M. Coats plantation on Mansker's Creek in Davidson County. Levi was about 35 and he stood about five feet tall. He wore large whiskers and was missing two fingers at the first joint. Evidently, they had been bitten off.

When he ran away, Levi was wearing a brown homespun jeans coatee.

Coats offered a $10 reward for Levi's return.

Source: *The Nashville Whig*, May 30, 1821.

June 18, 1821. Joseph and Robert Woods wanted to purchase four slaves. They were willing to pay cash for two boys between the ages of 13 and 16, and two girls between the ages of 12 and 15.

Source: *The Nashville Whig*, June 18, 1821.

July 11, 1821. A Nashvillian wanted to sell a slave. The slave was a "first rate" wooden barrel maker, and a good carpenter. The Nashvillian was willing to give credit for 90 days to the buyer.

Source: *The Nashville Whig*, July 11, 1821.

July 25, 1821. A. Fisk was moving his family from Nashville to Natchez, Mississippi, and he was selling his household and kitchen furniture. At the same time, he wanted to purchase three slaves. He wanted a woman who was a competent house servant and was not older than 22; a girl 13 or 14 who was suitable for caring for small children; and a boy between 12 and 13 to be a house servant.

Source: *The Nashville Whig*, July 25, 1821.

August 1, 1821. A Nashvillian wanted to purchase "a few" young slaves.

Source: *The Nashville Whig*, August 1, 1821.

August 13, 1821. David Shropshire jailed a slave named Jerry in Dickson County. Jerry was 25 or 26, and he stood about 5'9". He had a scar on his right cheek close to his nose caused by a bite, and he was light complexioned.

When he was arrested Jerry was wearing a short coat green in color, and a pair of blue-gray pantaloons.

Shropshire requested that anyone holding a claim to Jerry come to the jail and get him.

Source: *The Nashville Whig*, May 30, 1821.

September 5, 1821. The Tennessee State penitentiary in Nashville released its expenses between 1808 and 1820. The total was almost $500,000, and the only expenditures that drew any complaints were the amounts for slave rations ($1,206), and slave transportation ($2,120.68).

Source: *The Nashville Whig*, September 5, 1821.

September 30, 1821. Two slaves escaped from Charles Bosley's plantation about four miles from Nashville.

One slave was named Joe. He was about six feet tall and slender. He had a rough face and big feet.

When he left, Joe took two shirts, one brown linsey, and the other one cotton, a blue striped pair of pantaloons, a coat sewn from homemade cloth, a wool hat, and good shoes.

The other escaped slave was named Harry. He was about the same height as Joe. Harry walked on his toes, and he had big feet.

When he ran away, Harry took two shirts with him. One shirt was linen and the other one was cotton.

Joe and Harry had been delivered to Bosley's plantation from Richmond, Virginia just a few days before, and they ran away almost immediately.

Bosley expected them to try to get back there. He offered to reward the person bringing them back to him.

Source: *The Nashville Whig*, October 3, 1821.

October 4, 1821. Thomas Watson held a big sale on the west fork of Red River in Montgomery County seven miles north of Clarksville, and 18 miles south of Hopkinsville, Kentucky. The sale included a forge, a 1,700-acre plantation (160 acres cleared), a saw mill, a grist mill, a still producing 100 gallons of whiskey per day, and livestock.

Additionally, Watson also sold 20 slaves (men, women, boys, and girls). Some of the slaves were "valuable house servants." Watson demanded cash for the slaves.

Source: *The Nashville Whig*, July 4, 1821.

October 15, 1821. A slave named Phil got away from John Bressie's plantation on west fork of Goose Creek near Hartsville. Phil was 21-years-old, and he stood about 5'9". He had a light complexion, and his front teeth were decayed.

When he left, Phil was wearing, or carrying, a mixed cloth homespun coat, one pair of white jeans, a pair of pale corduroy pantaloons, and an old black broadcloth coat.

Bressie thought Phil would try to get to Ohio or Illinois. Bressie offered "reasonable compensation" to anyone that returned Phil to him.

Phil was captured and returned to the Bressie plantation, but he didn't abandon his desire to be free. More than 15 years later, he tried to escape again. On January 19, 1837, Elizabeth Bressie reported that Phil had escaped. By this time, his front teeth were missing. She believed that Phil, now past 35, would try to get to a Free State.

Bressie offered between $25 and $50 for his return, depending upon where he was found.

Sources: *The Nashville Whig*, October 24, 1821; *The Nashville Republican*, January 19, 1837.

October 16, 1821. John Cockrill of Davidson County petitioned the Tennessee legislature asking for the emancipation of two young slaves (Sam and Harry) in accordance with the Last Will and Testament of the late Thomas Mallory.

Source: Office of Tennessee Secretary of State, *Tennessee Legislative Petitions.*

October 16, 1821. The legislature received another petition requesting a law be passed which would allow slaveholders in Tennessee to emancipate their slaves if they so wished.

Source: Office of Tennessee Secretary of State, *Tennessee Legislative Petitions.*

November 15, 1821. The executors of the Craven Jackson estate sold all his property except for three slaves (two men and one woman). He hired them out until Christmas 1822.

Source: *The Nashville Whig,* November 15, 1821.

November 28, 1821. The Tennessee legislature passed a bill stating that if any slave were sold by court order to satisfy a debt, the purchaser had to provide security equal to twice the sales price of the slave before he could take possession.

Source: *The Nashville Whig,* November 28, 1821.

November 28, 1821. John L. Brown announced that he was going to ask the court in Wilson County to divide the slaves of the late Colonel Bedford Brown between the Colonel's heirs.

Source: *The Nashville Whig,* November 28, 1821.

December 10, 1821. A slave named Charles escaped from George Smith of Nashville. Charles was about 30 and he stood about 5'9". He was a plasterer by trade, and he could operate a printing press.

Smith was determined for no one to help Charles. Smith wrote, "All persons are forewarned from harboring, employing, or trading with him in any manner as the law will be put in force against persons so offending."

Smith offered a reward of $20 if Charles was jailed out of state, or $10 if he was detained in Tennessee. Smith promised to pay "reasonable charges" to anyone returning Charles to his property.

Source: *The Nashville Whig*, March 13, 1822.

December 15, 1821. Andrew Hays sold property on Mill Creek to settle the debts of John H. Lewis. Along with the 219-acre plantation, Hays sold three slaves, a woman and her two children. One child was seven or eight and the other one was four or five.

The sale fell through and Hays sold the property again on June 29, 1822.

Source: *The Nashville Whig*, October 24, 1821; *The Nashville Whig*, June 5, 1822.

December 19, 1821. Joseph Litton of the Golden Shoe Store on College Street in Nashville received a shipment of winter and spring goods. Included were strong work shoes made especially for slaves.

Source: *The Nashville Whig*, December 19, 1821.

December 22, 1821. Edward Ward hired out the slaves held by the estate of the late William Dickson at the Market-House in Nashville. He expected them to be returned in late December of 1822.

Source: *The Nashville Whig*, December 12, 1821.

December 24, 1821. Edward Ward hired out the slaves of the Peter Jones estate for the year 1822. He had prospective renters to meet at Sanders & Chandlers.

Source: *The Nashville Whig*, September 5, 1821.

December 29, 1821. R. C. Foster was the guardian for the heirs of the late John Camp. Foster held an auction at the Nashville

Courthouse where he rented 15 or 20 slaves for the 1822. Among the slaves were men, women, boys, and girls.

Source: *The Nashville Whig*, December 19, 1821.

1822

January 1, 1822. Peter and Sally Moseley rented several slaves for the entire year. Among them were men, women, and children.

Source: *The Nashville Whig*, November 14, 1821.

January 9, 1822. John Popp had properties for sale. He had 150 acres on Mill Creek in Davidson County, six miles southeast of Nashville. 70 of the acres were wooded. He had another 600 acres in Wilson County within five miles of Lebanon and one mile of the Cumberland River. Topp was willing to accept cash or slaves for the property.

Source: *The Nashville Whig*, January 9, 1822.

January 23, 1822. Mary Searcy was selling the plantations of the late Judge Searcy at Clarksville and Springfield. 550 acres in total were sold. Searcy was willing to take cash, store goods, or slaves as payment.

A young attorney named Cave Johnson handled the sale.

Source: *The Nashville Whig*, January 23, 1822.

Note: Cave Johnson (1793-1866) was a protégée of Andrew Jackson and James K. Polk, and he rose to become a prominent politician in his own right. Johnson served in the US House of Representatives and as Postmaster General of the United States. In 1844, Johnson received votes for President at the Democratic National Convention.

January 23, 1822. Christopher Robertson had his combination tavern/hotel in Charlotte, Tennessee for sale. The property was valuable because travelers from east and west passed it. Roberton was willing to accept cash, slaves, or other property for his building.

Source: *The Nashville Whig*, January 23, 1822.

February 13, 1822. Mordecai Pillow was selling 320 acres of land eight miles south of Mill Creek in Davidson County. He was willing to accept slaves as partial payment for the property.

Source: *The Nashville Whig*, April 17, 1822.

February 23, 1822. Three slaves, a woman and two children, were sold at the courthouse in Springfield to settle the debts of John Strother.

Source: *The Nashville Whig*, January 9, 1822.

March 1, 1822. The property of Richard Watkins in Wilson and Montgomery Counties was sold to pay his creditors. The property consisted of over 300 acres, livestock, and other items.

Also sold were eight slaves (men, women, and boys).

Source: *The Nashville Whig*, January 16, 1822.

March 27, 1822. A slave named Charles escaped from Colonel E. Ward's plantation In Davidson County. Charles was about 25, he stood about 5'7", was enormously powerful, had a large scar across his forehead, and a small blemish on one of his eyes.

The runaway's wife was enslaved on the plantation belonging to Alexander Walker on the north side of the Cumberland River near Haysboro. Ward claimed that several people had reported sighting Charles near the Walker place.

Ward offered $30 to anyone who returned Charles to him.

Source: *The Nashville Whig*, April 17, 1822.

April 7, 1822. Charles Bosley, who lived four miles south of Nashville, wanted to purchase "a few" young slaves between the ages of 14 and 22.

Source: *The Nashville Whig*, April 7, 1822.

April 11, 1822. A slave named Henry escaped from Z. Grant's plantation near Port Royal, Tennessee. Henry was about 20, and he stood about 5'9". Henry had a light complexion, and he bore a scar on his forehead near the hairline.

Grant purchased Henry from Jonathan Cowley in 1819 while Cowley was making his way from Virginia to Missouri.

Grant offered $25 for the return of Henry.

Source: *The Nashville Whig*, May 22, 1822.

May 1, 1822. The Campbell & Eastman company had nine slaves for sale. They promised to sell them cheaply, but he would only accept payment in cash.

Source: *The Nashville Whig*, May 1, 1822.

May 9, 1822. The property of the late Nathan Stancil was sold in accordance with his final wishes. Included in the sell were 16 slaves.

Source: *The Nashville Whig*, April 24, 1822.

May 11, 1822. By the order of the Davidson County court, J. P. Erwin sold four slaves that had been held by William Vaughn. The slaves were a man named Bob, a woman named Chana, and two boys, Henry and Jerry. Buyers were given 60 days to pay.

Source: *The Nashville Whig*, May 1, 1822.

June 11, 1822. A slave named Billy escaped from the Edward Jones plantation in Sumner County near Gallatin. Billy was between 35 and 40, and he stood about 5'8". Billy had a light complexion, and a full head of hair peppered with gray. Billy was fond of talking and laughing.

Billy had lived at taverns in Nashville and he was well known in the city. He had also driven a hack between Nashville and Louisville, Kentucky during the previous winter.

Jones offered $50 for Billy's return, or $25 if Billy was jailed and Jones had to retrieve him.

Source: *The Nashville Whig*, June 26, 1822.

June 19, 1822. C. Y. Hooper was selling 270 acres of land four miles north of Nashville, and two miles from Page's Ferry. Hooper wanted slaves as payment.

Source: *The Nashville Whig*, June 19, 1822.

August 4, 1822. Two slaves escaped from the David H. Harding plantation 10 miles southwest of Nashville.

One of the slaves was named Sam. He was about 27, and he stood about 5'10". Sam was a good fiddle player.

John was the other slave. He was about 22, he stood about 5'10", and he stuttered.

Harding purchased Sam in Virginia, and he bought John in Maryland. Harding believed the runaways would split up and each would try to return to his respective state of birth.

Harding was offering $25 each for Sam and John.

Source: *The Nashville Whig*, August 28, 1822.

August 5, 1822. A slave named John escaped from the Henry Robertson near Fayetteville. John was about 35, and he stood about six feet tall.

When he ran away, John was wearing white homespun pantaloons, a vest, and a white kersey roundabout coat.

Robertson had purchased John in Mississippi, but John said he had once belonged to a Nashvillian named Goffney. Robertson believed John would call himself John Goffney and try to pass himself off as a free man. Robertson offered a $20 reward to get John back.

Source: *The Nashville Whig*, September 4, 1822.

Note: Kersey is a coarse woolen cloth.

September 14, 1822. John H. Lewis was selling a slave held by Ernest Benoit in order to recoup the debt Benoit owned him. The slave was named Harry and he was 29-years-old.

Source: *The Nashville Whig*, August 28, 1822.

September 16, 1822. Dickson County jailer, William Bishop, lodged a slave named Sam in the jail at Charolette. Sam was between 20 and 25, and he stood about 5'6". Sam had extremely clear speech.

Sam said he belonged to a Mrs. Clinton of Bedford County prompting Bishop to request that she come forward, prove ownership, and take Sam away.

Source: *The Nashville Whig*, September 25, 1822.

September 20, 1822. A slave named Betty escaped from the John Strode plantation near Gallatin. Betty was about 40. She had a light complexion, and she was slender.

Strode offered a $20 reward to anyone who returned Betty to him from outside Tennessee, and $10 if she was captured within the state.

Source: *The Nashville Whig*, September 25, 1822.

September 25, 1822. A Nashvillian staying at the Nashville Inn wanted to purchase a slave boy between the ages of 12 and 15.

Source: *The Nashville Whig*, September 25, 1822.

October 1, 1822. A slave named Davy escaped from the Peter Moseley plantation on the Cumberland River 11 miles north of Nashville. Davy was between 35 and 40, and he stood about 5'7". Davy was a good shoemaker and he could read and write. Moseley had purchased Davy from Christopher Stump of Nashville in 1818 or 1819.

Davy's wife and children were enslaved on a plantation near Knoxville, and Moseley thought Davy might try to get to them. But, according to Moseley, Davy might also try to pass himself off as a free man and get to Ohio or another Free State.

Moseley promised that anyone who delivered Davy to him or detained the runaway slave would be "well-rewarded."

Source: *The Nashville Whig*, October 16, 1822.

October 16, 1822. In accordance with his final wishes, the entire estate of Colonel Osburne Jeffreys was sold at the Smith County Courthouse in Carthage. The Jeffreys property was quite substantial. It included a plantation of 477 acres of bottom land, 120 of which were cleared and fenced, with a two-story dwelling on it. He also had 20 other acres south of the Cumberland River. Several slaves were sold for cash as well.

Source: *The Nashville Whig*, September 11, 1822.

October 23, 1822. A Nashvillian had a young slave girl and her five-year-old child for sale.

Source: *The Nashville Whig*, October 23, 1822.

November 16, 1822. Nine slaves escaped in what authorities suspected to be a coordinated action in Bedford and Williamson Counties.

Three slaves escaped from Abraham Byler of Bedford County.

One slave was named Reuben. He was about 22 and he stood about 5'9".

When Reuben escaped, he was wearing a white waistcoat and a hat.

The other slaves that got away from Byler were Peggy and her son. Peggy was 19 or 20. She had a scar on one cheek.

When Peggy escaped, she was wearing a silk hat.

Peggy's son was four or five years old.

Two slaves escaped from a woman referred to a "widow" Nunn of Williamson County.

The slave, named Harry, was about 24, he stood about 5'10", and he was thin. One of his lower front teeth was missing. Harry could read and write.

A slave woman named Winnie also ran away from Nunn. Winnie was 18 or 19 and she had a light complexion.

Another slave named Penny and her three children (a boy and two girls) escaped from Nicholas Gentry. Penny was about 24-years-old and she was "a little cross-eyed."

The belief was that all nine escaped slaves would stay together and try to get to a Free State.

A liberal reward was offered for the return of the slaves.

Source: *The Nashville Whig*, November 20, 1822.

November 27, 1822. Peter Moseley had 804 acres of land on the Cumberland River north of Nashville. 250 acres were bottom land and 120 acres were cleared off for cultivation. Moseley was willing to take cash or slaves in payment.

Source: *The Nashville Whig*, December 4, 1822.

1823

January 25, 1823. Matthew Barrow, an agent for the Bank of Nashville, hired out a number of slaves to the highest bidders at the Courthouse in Nashville. There were men, women, boys, and girls hired out.

Source: *The Nashville Whig*, January 22, 1823.

February 6, 1823. A slave named Lizzy escaped from the Nashville plantation owned by S. V. P. Stout. Lizzy was about 28, and she stood about five feet tall. Lizzy was soft-spoken, she had large eyes, and some of her teeth were missing. When she ran away, she was wearing "domestic" clothes.

Stout offered $10 to get Lizzy returned to him.

Source: *The Nashville Whig*, February 12, 1823.

January 29, 1823. Eldridge B. Robertson and Sterling C. Robertson were selling a massive amount of property in Giles County. They were selling a plantation on Richard Creek which was between 5,000 and 6,000 acres in size. 4,000 acres were "good" for planting, and 400 acres were cleared and fenced. The property produced between 1,000 and 1,200 pounds of seed-cotton per cultivated acre.

They were also selling 35 slaves. Most of the slaves were under 40-years-old, some of them were good mechanics, and about 30 were fit for work in the cotton fields.

The Robertsons wanted $50,000 for the 4,000 acres of good land, the 35 slaves, livestock, and farming implements. They required $5,000 up front, and the rest in three equal annual payments. They weren't charging any interest.

Source: *The Nashville Whig*, January 29, 1823.

February 28, 1823. A slave named Ned escaped from the plantation owned by Theophilus Falls in Lawerence County. At 50, Ned was older than most runaways. He stood about 5'8", and he was slender. He wore short whiskers, which were gray. One or both of his ankles were larger than normal and this condition caused his feet to turn outward when he walked. Otherwise, he was rather ordinary looking.

When he departed, Ned took an old wool hat, a new pair of mixed cloth pantaloons, a new close bodied coat, an old pair of satin pantaloons, and an old coat with him.

Falls had purchased Ned in North Carolina during 1822, and he believed the runaway would either try to get back there, or to a Free State. Falls was also certain that if captured, Ned would never admit where he escaped from.

Source: *The Nashville Whig*, April 23, 1823.

March 2, 1823. A slave named Benjamin escaped from William Ward's plantation ten miles north of Murfreesboro. Benjamin was between 30 and 35. He was a big, tall "rough" looking man, and he had a long beard. However, he was well-spoken. Benjamin was also talented. He was a good shoemaker, a good hostler, and he understood flatboat building.

Ward offered a $10 reward if Benjamin was captured in Rutherford County, $20 if he was captured outside the county, but still in Tennessee, or $50 if captured outside Tennessee, and returned to the Ward farm.

Source: *The Nashville Whig*, April 23, 1823.

March 18, 1823. Pursuant to a Chancery Court order, seven slaves that had been held by the late Samuel Fleming were auctioned at Rock Springs in Bedford County. The slaves included males and females, and most of them were young.

Source: *The Nashville Whig*, February 5, 1823.

March 22, 1823. A slave named Silas escaped from John Tonelli's plantation located on the Franklin Road eight miles from Nashville. Silas was about 22, and he stood 5'6". He had a small head, full eyes, a wide mouth, and gaps between his teeth.

When he ran away, Silas was wearing a green roundabout cloth coat lined with red flannel, mixed material jean pantaloons, and a waistcoat. Silas took other garments with him and Tonelli believed the runaway had changed cloths soon after escaping.

Tonelli offered a $10 reward to anyone who returned Silas.

Source: *The Nashville Whig*, March 22, 1823.

March 31, 1823. Anthony W. Vanleer & Company was selling 30 slaves at the Tennessee Iron Works on Barton's Creek in Dickson County. The slaves were men and boys. Two were first-rate blacksmiths, and three were excellent waggoners.

Source: *The Nashville Whig*, March 26, 1823.

April 9, 1823. John L. Viser was selling two lots in Charlotte, Tennessee. One lot was on the town's Public Square. Viser let it be known that he would accept slaves in lieu of cash.

Source: *The Nashville Whig*, April 9, 1823.

April 30, 1823. On April 1, Henry Ashburn of Logan County, Kentucky hired out slaves to labor at Napier's Ironwork's in Dickson County, Tennessee. Then on April 30, two of the slaves Ashburn hired escaped, went back to Logan County, and were hiding out there.

One of the runaways was named Toby. He was about 35, he was of average height, homely looking, and he limped.

Toby took a considerable amount of clothing with him. He had a brown linen-frockcoat, two close-bodied coats, one black and the other white made of mixed materials. He had one or two pairs of double woven pantaloons and one cashmere pantaloons.

The other escaped slave was named Lewis. Lewis was of average height, skinny, light complexioned, and he stuttered.

Lewis had a long, dark plain linen coat that reached his ankles, two blue double woven linen coats, two pairs of linen pantaloons, one pair double woven, and one pair single woven. Additionally, he had one new pair of pantaloons, and one new shirt.

Ashburn felt Toby and Lewis would change clothes and would assume aliases. He also assumed that they would remain in Logan County for some time, and that they'd visit Russellville. Only after that, so thought Ashburn, Toby and Lewis would seek permanent freedom north of the Ohio River.

Ashburn offered $50 each for the runaways if they were captured more than 100 miles from Russellville and $25 each if they were arrested within 100 miles of the town.

Source: *The Nashville Whig*, April 30, 1823.

May 17, 1823. A slave named Charlie escaped from Thomas Cash's plantation nine miles south of Franklin, Tennessee. Charlie was about 21, he stood about 6'1", and he was thin. He had some upper teeth out, but he spoke freely. Charlie was artistic, and he was a good blacksmith.

Charlie had a brown broad cloth and "plenty of other clothing" with him when he left.

Cash had purchased Charlie from Reverend Gideon Blackburn of Williamson County, Tennessee, but he didn't think Charlie would go back there. Cash suspected that Charlie had gone to Nashville and had stowed away on the steamboat *Pittsburgh*. Cash believed that Charlie would try to get to Lexington, Kentucky and then, maybe, to go on to a Free State.

Cash offered $30 for Charlie's capture and return.

Source: *The Nashville Whig*, May 28, 1823.

June 10, 1823. In accordance with the last wishes of Absalom Page, 18 or 20 slaves (men, women, and children) were sold on the Public Square in Nashville.

Source: *The Nashville Whig*, April 30, 1823.

June 16, 1823. There was an estate sale at the home of the late Corbin Noles in Davidson County. Six slaves, a man, a woman, and four children were sold. The sellers gave buyers credit for one year.

Source: *The Nashville Whig*, June 4, 1823.

June 11, 1823. Andrew Hynes had possession of the promissory notes from those that had hired slaves from Charles H. Dickinson. Hynes demanded that they pay what they owed, otherwise he would bring legal action against them.

Source: *The Nashville Whig*, August 11, 1823.

June 23, 1823. A slave named Shawney and his wife Besty escaped from the plantation belonging to John Boyd.

Shawney was about 30, he stood about 5'10", and he weighed about 175 pounds. He was missing one of his upper front teeth, had a scar, perhaps made by a burn, on his right temple. He was stooped forward a little, and he walked with a slight limp. He was "fond of spirits." He had rudimentary reading and writing skills, was a good shoemaker, sawyer, and he excelled at farm work. He had grown up on the Boyd plantation and he had never been more than 50 miles from there.

Shawney took several articles of clothing with him. Among them were a blue jean coat, three shirts, one of which was made of coarse linen and was ruffled. He had three or four pairs of pantaloons, one pair of jeans, one pair of shoes, two pairs of coarse socks, an old woolen hat, and one or two black stripped waistcoats.

Besty was about 30, and she weighed about 120 pounds. Her complexion was so light, that she could have easily been mistaken for a white woman. In fact, she had passed herself off as a white woman in the past. Her eyes were "bluish gray" and there was a "film" or speck over one of them. Betsy had one or two decayed teeth and was a "great drunkard."

She was wearing a white sun bonnet and other clothes that she kept in a long basket with those that her husband brought along.

Besty had two daughters, one was 7 or 8 and the other one was 10 or 12. Boyd wasn't certain whether Besty's children were with her or not.

Boyd thought Shawnee and Betsy would begin their journey toward permanent freedom by going down the Cumberland, and then by trying to get to catch a boat to a Free State.

Boyd offered a $50 reward for Shawney, but nothing for Betsy. It may have been that Boyd didn't have any claim to Betsy, or it may have been that he just didn't want her back.

Source: *The Nashville Whig*, June 30, 1823.

August 18, 1823. Sumner County jailer Joshua Smith put out the word that he had a slave boy named Charles locked up in the jailhouse at Gallatin. Charles was about 5'5", and he was in his early teens.

Charles was wearing a broadcloth surcoat with a velvet collar. He said he belonged to James Jackson of Florence, Alabama.

Smith requested that Jackson come to Gallatin and retrieve Charles.

Source: *The Nashville Whig*, August 18, 1823.

September 9, 1823. Andrew Hays sold a slave woman and her two eldest children in Nashville. The purpose of the sale was to settle the debt due John H. Lewis from Jenkins Whiteside.

Source: *The Nashville Whig*, August 25, 1823.

September 29, 1823. J. Ragsdale of Williamson County asked the Tennessee legislature to compensate him for a slave named Jim. Jim suffered hanging by authorities on May 31 for a capital offense.

Source: *The Nashville Whig*, October 6, 1823.

November 17, 1823. Passage on steamboats from Nashville to New Orleans for whites was between $5 and $35. Additionally, each slave they took along cost an additional $2.

Source: *The Nashville Whig*, November 17, 1823.

November 22, 1823. Stewart County jailer, John Scarbrough, announced that he had locked up a slave named Bill. Bill had a light complexion, and he had a scar on his forehead.

Bill was wearing ordinary blue clothes.

Bill said he belonged to William Jones, formerly of Franklin, Georgia. He said he escaped while Jones was transporting him to Courtland, Alabama. Bill said that he and a slave named Dave had escaped from Jones somewhere near Tuscaloosa, Alabama.

Scarbrough believed that Dave may have traveled through Henry County and on to Stewart County, where he was arrested. However, his travels in Tennessee couldn't be confirmed.

Scarbrough requested that Jones come to the jail at Dover, prove he had title to Bill, and leave with the runaway.

Source: *The Nashville Whig*, December 8, 1823.

November 28, 1823. The late Thomas Sample's estate was sold in Davidson County. A slave Sample held was sold as well.

Source: *The Nashville Whig*, November 17, 1823.

December 20, 1823. Four slaves held by Nicholas H. Pryor were auctioned off at the courthouse in Nashville. The slaves were Helda, age about 26, and her two children Sophia and Amanda; and a slave woman named Betty, age about 38.

Source: *The Nashville Whig*, December 8, 1823.

1824

January 1, 1824. The slaves (men, women, and children) held by the estate of Colonel Bedford Brown were hired out for 12 months.

Source: *The Nashville Whig*, December 29, 1823.

January 1, 1824. The slaves (men, women, boys, and girls) of the minor heirs of the late James Camp were hired out at the courthouse in Nashville. The term of their hire was one year.

Source: *The Nashville Whig*, December 29, 1823.

January 2, 1824. The guardians of Joseph Caldwell's minor heirs hired to the highest bidders the slaves to which they held titles. The slaves were hired out until December 25, 1824.

Source: *The Nashville Whig*, December 22, 1823.

January 12, 1824. A slave named Bob escaped from the plantation owned by John H. Dolon on the Obion River in Henry County, Tennessee. Bob was about 30, he stood about 5'10", and he was physically "well-made." He wore a beard, and he had a scar on his nose and upper lip. He was a good barber, and he was an excellent hostler. He was also very polite.

Dolon promised to pay a $20 reward for Bob's return.

Source: *The Nashville Whig*, January 19, 1824.

January 13, 1824. The salt laden steamboat Telegraph while passing from the mouth of the Cumberland River "struck a snag and sank." The only causality was a slave who drowned.

Source: *The Nashville Whig*, January 19, 1824.

March 1, 1824. Duncan Robertson and Robert Sanderson agreed to dissolve their partnership. Sanderson continued the business with a new partner named Joseph Cowdin. Robertson went to business for himself selling slaves, real estate, horses, and other items.

Source: *The Nashville Whig*, March 1, 1824.

March 15, 1824. A slave named Henry escaped from Elijah Kimbrough's plantation in Rutherford County. Henry was about 22. He had been held previously held by the late Frederick Stump of Nashville.

Henry's wife was enslaved at N. A. McNairy's plantation in Davidson County and Kimbrough believed it was probable that Henry was trying to get to her.

Kimbrough promised a $10 reward to anyone that brought Henry to him, or $5 if Henry was captured but not delivered to the Kimbrough plantation.

Source: *The Nashville Whig*, May 3, 1824.

March 20, 1824. The Bank of Nashville, pursuant to an order of the Chancery Court, auctioned 34 slaves at the courthouse in Nashville. Buyers were given up to 18 months to pay. The heirs of the former slaveholder relinquished the right to the slaves and the sales were "absolute and unconditional."

Source: *The Nashville Whig*, March 8, 1824.

June 12, 1824. A slave named Morris escaped from the John Hays plantation on Mill Creek in Davidson County. Morris was about 40, but he looked much younger. He stood about six feet tall, and he had long hair. He was a "rough" shoemaker by trade.

When he left, Morris was wearing a blue broadcloth coat, a narrow-brimmed fur hat, and other clothing.

Hays believed that Morris had either gotten hold of a pass or that he had been taken away by a white man. Hays believed that Morris would either try to get to his wife in Alabama, or that he would attempt to get to a Free State.

Hays offered a $50 reward if Morris was captured out of state, or $25 if he was taken in Tennessee.

Source: *The Nashville Whig*, June 14, 1824.

June 18, 1824. James Boswell who lived near Shelbyville, arrested a man named Jacob and turned him over to Justice of the Peace M. D. Mitchell. Mitchell then had Jacob jailed on suspicion of being a runaway slave. Jacob was about 5'7", and he had a "stern visage."

When arrested, Jacob was wearing pantaloons made of blue cloth, and a black homespun coat. He denied that he was a slave, but he had nothing to prove he was a free man.

Oddly, Jacob told his captors that he was a fortune teller by trade.

Source: *The Nashville Whig*, July 12, 1824.

July 19, 1824. A Nashvillian wanted to hire a slave woman who was good at doing laundry and could iron well.

Source: *The Nashville Whig*, July 19, 1824.

August 25, 1824. Bedford County Justice of the Peace Giles Burdett ordered a young runaway slave named Ephraim to jail. Ephraim said he belonged to a man named Thomas Scott who lived near Huntsville, Alabama.

Sheriff John Wortham asked Scott to come to the jail and get Ephraim.

Source: *The Nashville Whig*, October 18, 1824.

October 7, 1824. Bedford County Justice of the Peace Robert Wallin ordered a young runaway slave named Henry to jail. Henry said he belonged to William or Samuel Gibbs of Warren County, Tennessee.

Sheriff John Wortham requested that any person with a claim for Henry come to the jail and get him.

Source: *The Nashville Whig*, October 7, 1824.

October 11, 1824. A slave named Billy escaped from the N. A. McNairy plantation near Nashville. Billy was about 35, he was average sized, and he had a light complexion.

Billy had been a servant at the Nashville Female Academy a few years before and he was well-known in the area.

McNairy offered a $50 reward to anyone who delivered Billy to him, or $25 if the runaway was found in Davidson County, and McNairy had to retrieve him.

Source: *The Nashville Whig*, October 11, 1824; *Nashville Whig*, January 17, 1825.

October 18, 1824. A Nashvillian had a slave woman for sale at what he said was a low price. She was accustomed to housework.

Source: *The Nashville Whig*, October 18, 1824.

November 1, 1824. News arrived in Tennessee that there had been a big political meeting at Sandy Mush, North Carolina in October. The dubious report stated that 73 people attended the meeting (20 men, 26 women, 17 girls, and 10 boys), and everyone was allowed to participate equally.

The message stated that a speaker promoting the candidacy of Secretary of State John Quincy Adams said that the son of the former President was a friend of the slaves and that if he were elected, he would emancipate them all.

The supposed vote for President at the meeting was as follows.:

Henry H. Crawford of Georgia: 24 (15 men, 5 women, 2 girls, and 2 boys).

Andrew Jackson, of Tennessee: 21 (10 women, 6 boys, and 4 girls, and 1 man).

Henry Clay, of Kentucky: 16 (6 girls, 5 women, 3 men, and 2 boys).

John Quincy Adams, of Massachusetts: 12 (6 women, 5 girls, and 1 man).

Source: *The Nashville Whig*, November 1, 1824.

December 2, 1824. The steamboat *Nashville* left Nashville for New Orleans. The ship was loaded with cotton, tobacco, candles, processed beef, and passengers. Additionally, 10 slaves were hustled aboard.

Source: *The Nashville Whig*, December 6, 1824.

October 13, 1824. A handcuffed slave named Fountain broke away from Lysander McGavock and escaped. Fountain stood about 5'8", he had a light complexion, and a broad face.

When Fountain escaped, he was wearing a small coatee, linen pantaloons, and an old, small-brimmed hat made from fur.

McGavock offered a $10 reward to anyone who delivered Fountain to him in Nashville.

Source: *The Nashville Whig*, November 8, 1824.

December 16, 1824. The Steamship *President* departed Nashville for New Orleans. It was loaded with various agricultural products, paying passengers, and slaves.

Source: *The Nashville Whig*, December 20, 1824.

1825

January 3, 1825. Nashville police officers were instructed to apprehend everyone Black person claiming to free who could not present proof of it. The city government was cracking down on slaves who were hiring themselves out as day laborers without the knowledge of their slaveholders. Slaves violating the law were to be jailed and their slaveholders were to be fined $8 and pay court costs for each offense.

The law was so strict that no slave could be in Nashville at any time without the slaveholder being there, or positive proof being presented that the slaveholder had hired out the slave.

Source: *The Nashville Whig*, January 3, 1825.

January 4, 1825. A slave named Quale escaped from Zach Wyatt's plantation at Dover in Stewart County, Tennessee. Quale stood about 5'10", he was knock kneed, and his upper front teeth were gapped. He was a first-rate distiller, as well as being a blacksmith.

When he ran away, Quale was wearing a "very strong pair of shoes with iron plates on the heels." He was also wearing dark colored pantaloons, and a hunting shirt had had new sleeves sewn on it.

Wyatt believed that either some white man had carried Quale off, or that the runaway had gotten a pass from someone. Wyatt promised a reward to the person returning Quale to him.

Source: *The Nashville Whig*, February 28, 1825.

January 18, 1825. Nine slaves that had been held by the late Roger B. Sappington were auctioned. The purpose of the sale was to relieve the Sappington estate it its debt. The sellers said that some of the slaves were "valuable men," and others were first rate house servants.

Source: *The Nashville Whig*, December 27, 1824.

January 19, 1825. Edward Ward offered to hire out to the highest bidders a number of slaves (men, women, boys, and girls) at Todd's Knob in Donelson, Davidson County.

Source: *The Nashville Whig*, January 17, 1825.

February 10, 1825. The trustees in charge of the late Alexander Richardson's estate sold its holdings to cover its debts. A slave girl was sold as part of the auction.

Source: *The Nashville Whig*, January 3, 1825.

February 14, 1825. A Nashvillian wanted to hire out two of his slaves. One was a man who was a good tanner and servant. The other one was a young woman who was a good worker.

Source: *The Nashville Whig*, February 14, 1825.

March 5, 1825. George Cockburn had parcels of land for sale in Columbia, Tennessee adjoining the town bridge. Cockburn was willing to accept bank notes or slaves for the property.

Source: *The Nashville Whig*, March 7, 1825.

April 2, 1825. A Nashvillian wanted to purchase a young male slave. He also had a slave girl that he wanted to hire out to someone.

Source: *The Nashville Whig*, April 2, 1825.

April 2, 1825. A slave named Billy escaped from the John Nichols plantation five miles south of Nashville. Billy was about 40, he stood about 5'6", and he was bowlegged. He had a light complexion, a straight black hair, and a scarified ear. He was fond of smoking his pipe, and of drinking whiskey.

Nichols thought Billy might try to pass himself off as a Native American, a Spainard, or a free Black man.

Nichols offered $50 for Billy if he was jailed out of state, and $25 if he was taken in Tennessee.

Source: *The Nashville Whig*, October 3, 1825.

April 5, 1825. John W. Marshall and others captured a slave named Henry in Eddyville, Kentucky and jailed him. Henry stood about 5'3", he had a light complexion, and he had a scar on his forehead. Henry was intelligent and he said he had been trained to be a house servant, and a hostler.

Henry said he belonged to John Trigg of Murfreesboro, Marshall wrote to Trigg, but Trigg hadn't responded. Marshall then requested that anyone with title to Henry come forward and claim him.

Source: *The Nashville Whig*, May 7, 1825.

April 23, 1825. Henry Crabb's plantation on the Cumberland River 10 miles North of Nashville was for sale or rent. The property included buildings, 90 acres capable of producing a cotton crop, and enough cotton seed to plant it. Crabb was willing to accept cash or slaves as payment.

Source: *The Nashville Whig*, April 23, 1825.

April 23, 1825. A slave named Willis escaped from the John G. Easley plantation in Vernon, Hickman County, Tennessee. Willis was between 40 and 45, and he stood about 5'6". He had a scar on one of cheeks, he walked briskly with his toes turned out.

Willis had often portrayed himself as a conjurer and fortune teller.

Easley thought Willis might be either in Murfreesboro, or somewhere else near Nashville. He offered $10 for the runaway's return.

Source: *The Nashville Whig*, April 23, 1825.

May 14, 1825. A slave named Jim who had run away from the Giles County plantation belonging to Tyree Rodes around 1822 was captured in Dickson County. When captured, Jum was riding a sorrel mare valued at $22.50. The horse's saddle and bridle were valued at $8. The belief was that Jim had acquired the horse and saddle honestly. However, just to be safe, the Dickson County Sheriff sent out word for anyone with a claim to the horse and saddle to contact him.

Source: *The Nashville Whig*, May 14, 1825.

May 28, 1825. Pursuant to a court order, the Sumner County Sheriff, Charles Morgan, auctioned off the property of Mary Herndon. Included in the sale was a male slave named Handy.

Source: *The Nashville Whig*, April 9, 1825.

June 11, 1825. A Nashvillian wanted to purchase a number of male slaves between 17 and 25 years of age.

Source: *The Nashville Whig*, June 11, 1825.

June 18, 1825. A Nashvillian wanted to purchase slaves. He said he was willing to pay a "liberal price" for them in cash.

Source: *The Nashville Whig*, October 3, 1825.

June 19, 1825. A slave named Charles (sometimes called Joe) escaped from the W. D. Whitsitt plantation in Henry County. Charles was 18 or 19.

Whitsett had purchased Charles from Dr. Joseph Minick near Nashville during the winter of 1824-1825, and he believed Charles would try to get a horse and get back to Nashville.

Whitsett was proven correct. Charles was captured and jailed in Nashville on July 1. He was returned to Henry County, but he soon escaped again.

Upon the second escape, Whitsett $10 for the return of the runaway.

Source: *The Nashville Whig*, July 16, 1825.

July 11, 1825. A slave named George escaped from the D. C. Ward plantation in Nashville. George was 19 or 20, and he stood about 5'8". George had a light complexion, a scar on his forehead above his left eye, and scars on his arms and legs he had gotten as a child. George was carpenter by trade.

George left wearing a brown surtout broadcloth coat, a black fur hat, and coarse shoes. He also had several changes of clothes with him.

George could read and write, and Ward thought the runaway might try to get or forge a pass that allowed him to travel unmolested. Ward believed that George would then try to get either to Smith County or to a Free State.

Ward was offering between $10 and $25 in award money, depending upon where George was captured ($25 if captured out of state, and $10 if captured within).

Source: *The Nashville Whig*, July 16, 1825.

July 22, 1825. A slave named Abraham escaped from George Malone in Giles County. Abraham was about 30, and he stood about 5'3". Abraham had a stiff ankle which caused him to limp.

When he left, Abraham was wearing homespun clothes.

Malone was offering a $30 reward if Abraham was captured in a Free State, or in another state outside Tennessee. The reward for an instate capture was $20.

Source: *The Nashville Whig*, October 3, 1825.

July 31, 1825. Five slaves escaped from the Isaac Franklin plantation at Station Camp in Sumner County.

Bradly, who was between 30 and 35, he stood about 6 feet tall, and he was slim. Bradley had a light complexion, a high forehead, maintained a pleasant expression, and was deliberate in his speech.

Sedrick was about 5'6" and he was "rather homely." His hair came down to his eyebrows.

Bill was about 35, and he stood about 5'8". He was slender, had a high forehead, and he wore a beard.

Elias was about 25, and he stood about 5'8". Elias smiled most of the time.

Alfred was about 19. He was smooth-faced, handsome, slim, and pleasant.

Franklin offered to pay a $25 reward for each slave if they were captured in either Sumner, Smith, Davidson, or Robertson counties. The reward went up to $50 for each slave captured in Kentucky, and "reasonable charges" if they were returned from a Free State.

Source: *The Nashville Whig*, August 6, 1825.

August 12, 1825. James Powell of Smith County reported that his wife, Sarah, had left him. When she left, Sarah took several valuable items with her, including $100 in promissory notes, and a slave woman.

Powell believed that some of Sarah's friends had convinced her to leave him in an attempt to injure or ruin him. He warned everyone not to aid his wife in any way.

Source: *The Nashville Whig*, August 13, 1825.

August 20, 1825. A slave named Sam escaped from the Asaph Alsup plantation at Fall Creek in Wilson County. Sam was about 17, and one of his front teeth was broken.

Sam was wearing a mixed-cloth homespun coat, blue jean pantaloons, and a black fur hat.

Alsup promised to reward anyone who returned Sam to him.

Source: *The Nashville Whig*, August 20, 1825.

September 4, 1825. Two slaves escaped from Charles Bosley's plantation four miles from Nashville.

One slave was named Isaac. He was about 27 and he stood roughly six feet tall. Isaac was light complexioned, and he had a scar shaped like a cross on his forehead just below his hairline.

When he ran off, Isaac was wearing a new flax linen shirt, a new pair of pantaloons made from the same material, and a new wool hat with a large brim. He took with him two checkered roundabouts, a pair of striped cotton pantaloons, and other garments.

The other slave was named Paddy. He was about 20, and he stood about 5'10". Paddy had large eyes, a narrow forehead, and a burn scar on his head.

Paddy left wearing a new wool hat with a large brim, a new pair of linen pantaloons, and a checkered shirt. He was also carrying a pair of old pantaloon, a linen shirt, and a white runabout.

Bosley had purchased the slaves from Lemuel Chadwick and Java Conduitt of Henderson County, Kentucky on August 23. He believed they might try to get back there.

Bosley believed the two runaways had perhaps $30 or $40 in cash with them.

Bosley offered $25 each for the runaways if they were caught in Tennessee, $50 if they were detained in Kentucky, and $100 if they were arrested elsewhere.

Source: *The Nashville Whig*, October 3, 1825.

September 6, 1825. Davidson County jailer, Edward Daniel, locked up a slave named Peter. At about 60, Peter was older than most runaways were. Peter stood about six feet tall; his left eye was smaller than his right eye; and his left little finger was crooked. He said he belonged to Peter Armistead of Lauderdale County, Alabama, about 5 miles from Florence.

Daniel requested that anyone with a claim to Peter come to Nashville and retrieve him.

Source: *The Nashville Whig*, September 17, 1825.

September 8, 1825. A slave was detained in Gallatin and locked up in the Sumner County jail. The slave was about 35, and he stood about 5'6". He said he belonged to Peter Armistead of Lauderdale County, Alabama.

It isn't certain, but it is possible that this slave escaped from Armistead with the slave Peter who was mentioned earlier.

Jailer J. D. Tompkins requested that anyone with a claim to the slave come to Nashville and retrieve him.

Source: *The Nashville Whig*, September 17, 1825.

September 11, 1825. Another slave escaped from the John Nichols plantation. Jacob was about 45 and he stood about 5'8". Jacob had a scar on his forehead from a cut. He was a carpenter by trade, and he was extremely confident and well spoken.

When he left, Jacob was wearing a white wool hat, a mixed cloth coat, and mixed cloth cassinette pantaloons. He took a white roundabout and white pantaloons with him as well.

Nichols offered $50 for Jacob if he was jailed out of state, and $25 if he was taken in Tennessee.

Source: *The Nashville Whig*, September 11, 1825.

Note: Cassinette pantaloons were lightweight twilled pants of wool-filled cotton.

September 12, 1825. A slave named George escaped from the John Frost plantation 10 miles South of Nashville. George was about 21, and he stood about 5'8". George was smart and Frost thought the runaway slave would try to get to a Free State.

Frost offered a $25 reward for George's return.

Source: *The Nashville Whig*, September 17, 1825.

September 19. A slave named Hance escaped from the plantation belonging to William W. Hamon in Maury County. Hance stood about 5" 9", and he weighed about 175 pounds. Hance had long, straight hair, his teeth were defective, and his hands and feet were large. When he ran away, Hance was wearing a cotton coat and pantaloons, and a black silk vest with no buttons.

Hamon offered $10 for Hance's return.

Source: *The Nashville Whig*, October 10, 1825.

September 19, 1825. A petition bearing 235 signatures requested that the Tennessee legislature emancipate the slaves held within its borders.

Source: Office of Tennessee Secretary of State, *Tennessee Legislative Petitions*.

September 19, 1825. The legislature received another petition requesting that it emancipate aa the slaves in Tennessee. Many signatures were affixed to the petition.

Source: Office of Tennessee Secretary of State, *Tennessee Legislative Petitions.*

September 19, 1825. The legislature received a petition from Wayne County. The heirs of the late John Atkins requested that Tennessee lawmakers set free certain slaves in accordance with his wishes as they were expressed in his Last Will and Testament.

Source: Office of Tennessee Secretary of State, *Tennessee Legislative Petitions.*

September 19, 1825. A petition from Knox County, signed by many people, requested that the legislature emancipate slaves in Tennessee.

Source: Office of Tennessee Secretary of State, *Tennessee Legislative Petitions.*

September 19, 1825. The Manumission Society of Tennessee, located in Jefferson County, asked the lawmakers in Nashville to emancipate the slaves in the state.

Source: Office of Tennessee Secretary of State, *Tennessee Legislative Petitions.*

September 19, 1825. A petition signed by 36 people asked for the emancipation of Tennessee's slaves.

Source: Office of Tennessee Secretary of State, *Tennessee Legislative Petitions.*

September 19, 1825. A petition with 11 pages of signatures attached, requested that the Tennessee legislature emancipate slaves.

Source: Office of Tennessee Secretary of State, *Tennessee Legislative Petitions.*

September 19, 1825. Jabez J. Mitchell, the jailer of White County, requested to release a Black person who had been locked up in Sparta suspected of being a runaway slave. Mitchell's petition related that he had not located anyone claiming ownership of the man, and that no one had come forward, with proof of ownership.

Since there was no evidence that the imprisoned man was a slave, Mitchell asked the legislature to allow him to release the suspected slave.

Source: Office of Tennessee Secretary of State, *Tennessee Legislative Petitions*.

September 19, 1825. A petition from Anderson County was presented to Tennessee lawmakers. It proposed the abolition of slavery un the state.

Source: Office of Tennessee Secretary of State, *Tennessee Legislative Petitions*.

September 19, 1825. Another petition was presented to the legislature requesting the abolition of slavery in Tennessee.

Source: Office of Tennessee Secretary of State, *Tennessee Legislative Petitions*.

September 19, 1825. The Tennessee legislature received still another petition requesting the emancipation of slaves in the state.

Source: Office of Tennessee Secretary of State, *Tennessee Legislative Petitions*.

September 24, 1825. Davidson County jailer, Edward Daniel, confined a slave named Randal in the local lock up. Randal was about 5'6", and he was missing some of his upper and lower teeth.

Randal said he belonged to Henry Chambers of Big Prairie, Limestone County, Alabama.

Daniel requested Chambers, if he truly had legal title to Randal, to come to Nashville, secure the slave, and take him back to Alabama.

Source: *The Nashville Whig*, October 3, 1825.

September 26, 1825. A slave named Elijah (often called "Lige") escaped from Henry Crabb's plantation near Nashville. Elijah was over 35-years-old, and he stood about 5'10". He was bald in front, had a scar in the bald area, had stooped shoulders, and he spoke slowly.

Crabb believed that Elijah might have obtained a forged pass or that he might be pretending to be a free man. Crabb felt that Elijah might still be in the Nashville area or that he might be trying to get to Ohio.

Crabb offered a $50 reward for Elijah's capture and return.

Source: *The Nashville Whig*, October 3, 1825.

October 5, 1825. Davidson County jailer, Edward Daniel, was having a busy year. The latest slave the jailer incarcerated was named Isaac. Isaac was about 35, he had a scar on the back of his right hand, and a black spot on one of his upper front teeth.

Isaac said he belonged to John Eblin of Roane County, six miles from South West Point, Tennessee.

Daniel asked Eblin to come to Nashville and take possession of Issac.

Source: *The Nashville Whig*, October 10, 1825.

October 17, 1825. A slave named Moses escaped from Edward Childress in Nashville. Moses was about 30, and he stood about 5'10". According to Childress, Moses was fond of whiskey.

When he ran away, Moses was wearing a linsey coatee and linsey pantaloons.

Moses had a wife enslaved in Georgetown, Kentucky and Childress was certain that the runaway would try to get to her.

Childress was offering a $50 reward if Moses was returned from outside of Tennessee, and $20 if he was detained in the state. Moses was captured shortly thereafter, only to escape again (See November 1, 1825).

Source: *The Nashville Whig*, October 31, 1825.

October 31, 1825. Edward Daniel lodged still another escaped slave in the Davidson County jail. This slave, named William, was listed as being about 6'7". He had an upper front tooth broken out.

William said he belonged to a Captain Betts of Madison County, Alabama, and had previously been held by Matthew Jeffers of Frankfort, Kentucky.

Daniel requested that Betts make his way to Nashville, pay the jail fees, and take William away.

Source: *The Nashville Whig*, October 31, 1825.

November 1, 1825. Three slaves escaped from Nashville slave dealers, Daniel A. Dunham, William E. Watkins, and Edwin H. Childress:

Cato was about 28, he stood about 5'8", and he was slender. Cato was smart, and he could read and write. He had good manners, and he was a good conversationist. He was a blacksmith by trade. He had been formerly held by James Weir of Greenville, Kentucky.

Cato had recently suffered a severe axe wound to the top of his left foot.

Robin (also called Bob) was about 25. He was heavyset, and he stood about six feet tall. He had wide cheekbones and he was pleasant in speech.

Robin was wearing a silver-colored pair of pantaloons with eight buttons on the side of each pant leg near the ankle. Additionally, he had a blue broad cloth surtout coat and other articles of clothing with him.

Moses was wearing a white linen coatee, and a pair of linsey pantaloons. He had escaped earlier in the year and had been recaptured (See October 17, 1825).

The runaways were thought to be together and it was believed that they would endeavor to get to Indiana or Illinois.

The slaveholders offered $50 each for the slaves if they were caught outside of Tennessee, and $25 each if they were taken within the state.

Source: *The Nashville Whig*, November 7, 1825.

November 2. The Tennessee legislature considered a bill designed to pay slaveholders two-thirds of a slave's value if the slave was executed for a capital crime. The funds for the payments would be raised by an additional tax on slaveholders.

Source: *The Nashville Whig*, November 7, 1825.

November 16. The State House of Representatives considered and rejected a bill from the Senate that would have prevented human traffickers from transporting slaves from one state, across Tennessee, and on to another state.

Source: *The Nashville Whig*, November 21, 1825.

November 16. Sumner County jailer, John Tompkins, lodged another escaped slave in the county prison. The slave was light complexioned, and he wore a truss. He said he belonged to James Erwin who had purchased him from William Ward.

Tompkins requested Erwin to come to the jail at Gallatin and collect the slave.

Source: *The Nashville Whig*, November 21, 1825.

November 21. The Tennessee legislature adopted a law that allowed a slaveholder to attend trials of their slaves.

They could also challenge the seating of jurors in cases involving their slaves. However, the law only applied to slaves being tried for capital offenses. All jurors in such cases had to be slaveholders.

The law allowed a slaveholder to make bail for his accused slave in bailable cases. The bail was set at twice the value of the accused slave.

Slaveholders could appeal the convictions of their slaves, but they were to pay all costs unless they could prove the prosecution was "frivolous."

The legislature also amended the "patrol law" by mandating that slaves would "not be allowed to on the premises of another person at unlawful hours, or on Sunday, without a pass." Slaves were "subject to chastisement for doing so." Naturally, the term "chastisement" meant whipping.

Sources: *The Nashville Whig*, November 21, 1825; *The Nashville Whig*, December 5, 1825; *The Nashville Whig*, December 12, 1825; *The Macon County Times*, January 4, 1950.

Note: The state of Tennessee employed militiamen referred to as "patrollers." They were augmented by local patrols, of volunteers. Their principal functions were:

1. To keep a lookout for runaway slaves, and to make sure they didn't escape to their freedom.
2. To monitor the movements and activities of both slaves and free Black people.
3. To identify and prevent possible slave uprisings.

December 1. Most of the personal estate of late Richard Boyd was auctioned in Davidson County. However, 15 or 16 slaves held by the estate were not sold. They were hired out until the end of 1826.

Source: *The Nashville Whig*, November 21, 1825.

December 12. William Compton desired to pay cash for a few men and women slaves "of good character." Compton assured prospective sellers that the slaves wouldn't be taken out of the area, and that the slaves would be "treated with more than usual humanity."

Source: *The Nashville Whig*, December 12, 1825.

December 20. Joseph M. Bullos sold two slaves at the courthouse in Nashville. One slave was a woman and the other was a boy. Bullos declined to accept any payment other than cash.

Source: *The Nashville Whig*, December 5, 1825.

From the Author

The business of slavery in Middle Tennessee isn't a very pleasant topic. However, it is an important one. No one can be truly educated without delving into uncomfortable areas and investigating disturbing topics.

Learning about the magnitude of the slave business is vital in understanding America before, during, and after, the Civil War. It is doubtless that many of the challenges our great nation faces today are directly tied to the buying and selling human beings many years ago.

Again, this is not a happy topic, but it needs to be discussed in an open way, without any varnish or any rationalization.

Volume 2 will continue this story as the United States and will follow it until legal slavery finally after the bloodiest war in American history.

About the Author

CL Gammon has had a life-long fascination with the written word. This fascination has led to his authoring more than 70 books.

Gammon, studied Political Science at Tennessee Technological University and History and Government at Hillsdale College

Over the years, Gammon has received several prestigious honors and awards. He has twice received the Certificate of Appreciation for Service to the State of Tennessee (2018 and 2025), the Partisan Prohibition Historical Society Citation of Merit (the only two-time recipient), and nomination for the 2023 Gilder Lehrman Lincoln Prize.

Several universities, including the State University of New York, the University of Akron, and East Mississippi Community College, have utilized his books as course material.

Articles written by Gammon have appeared in more than a dozen national and regional publications. He has also written feature articles for his hometown newspaper, *The Macon County Times*.

CL Gammon lives in Lafayette, Tennessee.

www.ingramcontent.com/pod-product-compliance
Lightning Source LLC
Chambersburg PA
CBHW060805050426
42449CB00008B/1554